Praise for *Songs in the Night*

Songs in the Night is a practical, pastoral, warm, and extremely readable book that can be of immense help to readers. Its brief fourteen chapters are challenging and God-exalting, with ample testimony to God's amazing saving, keeping, and restoring grace. This is a book you must buy and pray over as you read it.

> —**D. Eryl Davies,** Head of Research, Wales Evangelical School of Theology

When you pick up a book and consider whether you want to read it, it helps to know whether the author knows what he or she is talking about, especially if the subject is suffering. Reading Mike's book won me immediately. You can tell that Mike has been a pastor and someone who has suffered personally. Pastors and sufferers can never be content with a theoretical answer to suffering. You must wisely develop a practical theology of suffering. *Songs in the Night* is just that. The main reason is because it is deeply rooted in Scripture and focused clearly on our suffering and triumphant Redeemer, Jesus.

> —**Tim Lane,** President, The Christian Counseling and Educational Foundation

SONGS IN
THE NIGHT

SONGS IN THE NIGHT

HOW GOD TRANSFORMS OUR PAIN TO PRAISE

MICHAEL A. MILTON

P U B L I S H I N G
P.O. BOX 817 • PHILLIPSBURG • NEW JERSEY 08865-0817

Unless otherwise indicated, Scripture quotations are from *ESV Bible* ® (*The Holy Bible, English Standard Version* ®). Copyright © 2001 by Crossway Bibles, a publishing ministry of Good News Publishers. Used by permission. All rights reserved.

Scripture quotations marked (NIV) are from the HOLY BIBLE, NEW INTERNATIONAL VERSION®. NIV®. Copyright © 1973, 1978, 1984 by International Bible Society. Used by permission of Zondervan Publishing House. All rights reserved.

Scripture quotations marked (NKJV) are from The Holy Bible, New King James Version. Copyright © 1979, 1980, 1982, Thomas Nelson, Inc.

Printed in the United States of America

Library of Congress Cataloging-in-Publication Data

Milton, Michael A. (Michael Anthony), 1958-
  Songs in the night : how God transforms our pain to praise / Michael A. Milton.
      p. cm.
  Includes bibliographical references.
  ISBN 978-1-59638-221-3 (pbk.)
  1. Suffering--Religious aspects--Christianity--Sermons. 2. Suffering--Biblical teaching. 3. Sermons, American. I. Title.
  BT732.7.M545 2011
  248.8'6--dc23
                                            2011031840

In memory of my mentor and friend,
Dr. D. James Kennedy,

And always to my wife,
Mae,

And to the Savior
who ever lives to intercede for His own

"Where is God my Maker,
who gives songs in the night?"
(Job 35:10)

CONTENTS

CONTENTS

PREFACE

What does a Roman Catholic priest, wresting with alcoholism and his own depravity, have to do with an evangelical Anglican in an eighteenth-century English village, trying to work out the glory of God in the grit of daily parish life? Or with a Presbyterian minister as he wrestles with serving a seminary and making sense of God's grace in the midst of his own shortcomings and the challenges of seeking to preach the gospel faithfully in the presence of others in their own struggles? The answer: our humanity and God's redemptive work in the midst of it.

When I read Brennan Manning's line years ago, "to whisper a doxology in the darkness," I knew I would write a collection of messages on this—more on the theme of the phrase than on the phrase itself, though you can see that I have kept the phrase as one of my chapter titles. This theme, which I called "songs in the night,"[1] has often been my theme in preaching since I heard Dr. James M. Baird tell us seminary students, paraphrasing Joseph Parker, "Boys, always preach to broken hearts and you will never lack for a congregation." I took Jim Baird at his word, and he was right. I have always assumed that the flock before me was wrestling with the same demons that I have had to deal with: sickness in my life or in the lives of my loved ones, spiritual depression, disabilities, painful memories, strained relationships (often in the body of Christ), and yet, in the midst of it all, a crying of the soul for eternity, for a new heavens and a new earth. Yet I have also assumed that a supernatural faith comes from Jesus Christ and works through the very things that seek to attack us, transforming our pain into praise. This is what Paul was writing about in "the great Eighth":

> Who shall separate us from the love of Christ? Shall tribulation, or distress, or persecution, or famine, or nakedness, or danger, or sword? As it is written, "For your sake we are being killed all the day long; we are regarded as sheep to be slaughtered." No, in all these things we are more than conquerors through him who loved us. For I am sure that neither death nor life, nor angels nor rulers, nor things present nor things to come, nor powers, nor height nor depth, nor anything else in all creation, will be able to separate us from the love of God in Christ Jesus our Lord. (Rom. 8:35–39)

"In all these things," Paul writes. And I have named those things, from our common experiences, and sought to minister the balm of the gospel I found here. "We are more than conquerors." That is not a Stoic affirmation of our own strength, or a detached, holier-than-thou, super-spiritual statement of a faith that doesn't match the reality of suffering. It is rather a song in the night. Those assumptions and that core faith in the truth of the gospel, the ruling motif of the cross and the empty tomb, form both the contents and the progression of chapters in this book. Each chapter concludes with questions for reflection—each still dealing with this core theme, this "musical note" of calming redemption in the terrifying night.

I have often heard people sing songs in the night in the most unusual places: funeral homes, hospitals, prisons, and oncology wards. I have heard them sung by a young officer after receiving the news that he was passed over for promotion and would be ousted from the military. I have heard this song, familiar but strange, sung in all of its paradoxical power by families gathered around their sweet, elderly mother as she was dying before their very eyes. I have heard this song as Haitian refugees sang the doxology with almost ethereal joy, after having lost everything in the horrible earthquake including, for some of them, their own children. How do we sing songs in the night?

This is the power of the cross. And my prayer is that this book will help you learn how to sing the doxology in the darkness, the songs in the night. That is not an acquired skill; it is a supernatural act of faith that is a gift from God. It does not come naturally. But it can come to each of us. As we draw near to God, he will draw near to us (James 4:8). My prayer is that as you read each chapter, reflect on each question, and consider each Scripture, you will draw near to God. Look to the Lord Jesus Christ, his life lived for you and his death providing atonement for you, when by grace you trust in him alone for eternal life. In him you will find the one who cried, "My God, my God, why have you forsaken me?" as he hung from the cross erected by the very people he created. You will see that the cross is the place where the fallen world, personal crises, physical challenges, painful memories, and broken relationships are transformed into a future hope of redemption, healing, and reconciliation. In that place you will cry out with alcoholics, prostitutes, preachers and seminary presidents, cancer patients, caregivers, moms and dads, college students, and struggling teens, with me and millions of others who long for God in the midst of "all these things" and give voice to the gift of faith with you. That is a doxology in the darkness, which is simply, poignantly, and powerfully the gospel at work in the world today.

Let me leave with you these words from *Morning and Evening* on Deuteronomy 5:24 by Charles Haddon Spurgeon, a preacher who through his preaching and writing ministry helps us today with our doxology in the darkness:

> He whose life is one even and smooth path, will see but little of the glory of the Lord, for he has few occasions of self-emptying, and hence, but little fitness for being filled with the revelation of God. They who navigate little streams and shallow creeks, know but little of the God of tempests; but they who do business in great waters, these see his wonders in the deep. Among the huge Atlantic-waves of bereavement, poverty, temptation, and reproach, we learn the power of Jehovah, because we feel the littleness of man.

Thank God, then, if you have been led along a rough road: it is this which has given you your experience of God's greatness and loving-kindness. Your troubles have enriched you with a wealth of knowledge to be gained by no other means. Your trials have been the cleft of the rock in which Jehovah has set you, as he did his servant Moses, that you might behold his glory as it passed by. Praise God that you have not been left to the darkness and ignorance that continued prosperity might have involved, but that, in the great fight of affliction, you have been shaped for the outshinings of his glory in his wonderful dealings with you.

ACKNOWLEDGMENTS

*"I may be tempted often enough to dim down
the light of faith and play for the safety of
a dumb conventional religion. But, thank
heaven, there is a Voice that won't ever let
me forget—You are Christ's man, and that
is the one great fact. Let the world deride or
pity. I will glory in His Name!"*[1]

As this book was being put together, friends from all over would not let me forget that this was not just another conventional religious book. As the chapters came together, there was a voice, and I believe it was the voice of the Lord, speaking through many people and congregations who were saying, "These messages must be given to the Church, for there are so many hurting people!" They were also saying, "Help us to discover his glory in the midst of these trials!"

I listened to his voice through congregations where I have recently had the privilege of preaching: First Presbyterian Church of Chattanooga, Tennessee; First Presbyterian Church of Jackson, Mississippi; Christ Covenant Church (PCA) in Matthews, North Carolina; First Presbyterian Church of Hattiesburg, Mississippi; New Presbyterian Church of Pompano Beach, Florida; Potomac Hills Presbyterian Church outside of Washington, D.C.; Parish Presbyterian Church of Franklin, Tennessee; the Cedar Falls Bible Conference; and the students of Reformed Theological Seminary, Charlotte and Orlando, as I preached in the chapels there.

I preached these messages and then edited them before chaplains, mission conferences, and spiritual retreats. There were many who contributed to this book by their witness of faith in Christ Jesus. So many churches, so many pastors, so many saints. I have heard the voice of the Lord through you, encouraging me to go on.

I am thankful for the work of Miss Helen Holbrook, for her editing and work in "stitching" together the messages into chapters. She generally did this while preparing for the next preaching trip, or helping put together the next report, or handling my travel arrangements or expense account! Thank you, Helen. I am deeply grateful to Mrs. Teresa Gillis, who wrote all of the "Questions for Reflection" following the chapters. I found that her questions caused me to return to the chapters myself and to answer her questions in my own life. As I was elected to become chancellor of Reformed Theological Seminary during the time of preparing this book, I was greatly aided by my assistant Wendy Simmons. In this, too, I heard the Lord's voice in this book.

I want to thank Reverend Ken McMullen, my trusted colleague, brother in the ministry, and gifted librarian at RTS, as well as a number of our diligent RTS Charlotte students, who, with Wendy, put up a gallant, last-minute effort to search out and insert several missing citations in the manuscript. In an age of "the digital revolution," to know that my assistant, seminary students and faculty still take time to rummage through the "parchments" is to keep the ancient Celtic candles of fifth century Irish monastics burning brightly! You give us hope! Thank you all.

I am grateful to the great team at P&R Publishing. Marvin Padgett, Ian Thompson, and Aaron Gottier have helped me remember the vision of this book, the audience for this book, and the excellence that is our goal.

I am thankful to the countless people who responded to these messages at the Communion table, at the front door, through e-mail or Facebook, on the phone, or in my office. Each of you was used of the Lord to become his voice to me in the preparation of this book.

I would be negligent if I did not say how encouraged I have been by my predecessor at Reformed Theological Seminary, Dr. Ric Cannada, and by my chief of staff and the chief operating officer of RTS, the Rev. Steve Wallace, who always encouraged me to go forward to preach the unsearchable riches of Christ. Indeed, I am associated with an extraordinary team at Reformed Theological Seminary. The Executive Committee, the Board of Trustees, faculty, presidents, and staff of all of our campuses have helped me. Much of this was written while I was serving RTS Charlotte, where I was president. My colleagues there always supported and encouraged me in my work of writing and preaching. Thanks to the cabinet members: Rod Culbertson, Charlie Dunn, Steve Halvorson, Stephane Jeanrenaud, and Mike Kruger for running the shop while I preach the Word and write and carry on the work of the seminary presidency through communication. RTS

Orlando, where I was interim president during most of the time, also helped me in many ways, particularly the Rev. Lyn Perez, who wears so many hats. Thanks also to Cristi Mansfield, Ceci Helm, Dawn Kilgore, Mark Futato, and so many others who provided administrative assistance as I wrote this work and also sought to serve the seminary in Orlando.

As I wind my way through the days of life and ministry, I want to thank all of our children and their children. To be your father and your "Poppy" is a great blessing and you will never know how your love encourages me to offer ministry to others. Thank you, children.

The Lord gave me a darkness to sing through as I was completing this work. I grew very ill with a mysterious malady having to do with neurological issues, heart rate, and what became a perfect storm of fatigue, virus and other things afflicting me. I learned again (for we all need to keep learning the lessons of faith, don't we?) that one can sing songs in the night in the midst of a frail body. God brought healing during this time and I am better now than I have been in over a year. There were no lasting consequences of the sickness. Yet it grew so severe that I was forced to take medical leave. I thank the Board for giving me that time and for my colleagues who all stepped up to encourage and pray for me. I learned that songs in the night are really sung best by a chorus of the church and not as a solo. I want to thank Dr. David Robertson of Vanderbilt Medical Center and Drs. David Framm, Chester Alexander, and Steven Putnum in Charlotte. Thanks also to the very kind and helpful nursing staff of the Vanderbilt Autonomic Dysfunction Center—

some of whose songs in the night I was able to learn as well as I was blessed by the care of Gina and the other wonderful professionals there.

I know afresh what "in sickness and in health" means because of my blessed Mae, who more than any single person nursed me to health. I did not deserve to be healed. I do not know why I was healed and others are not. I hope I would have praised the name of the Great Physician either way. I do give him my life again in this new season of thankfulness.

My wife and son listened to or read through every one of these messages before anyone else ever heard them or read them. Their presence is always a means of the Lord that will not allow my work to "be tempted to dim down the light of faith" in my life and ministry. I want to take this opportunity to say something special to both of them. Thank you, John Michael. You are growing to be a man now. Soon you will depart for college. Soon, very soon, you will begin to find God's answers in reality to God's impressions in your dreams. You will never know the joy you bring, which is always stoking the furnace of faith in my life. Thank you, Mae. My beloved bride, Mae, I honor you now as the best life-companion a man could ever desire. It is easy for me to say, "My wife is the heroine in the story of my life." You are. You encourage me to preach and to write, and your own faith nudges me forward to take a stand to say with the Scottish preacher, James Stewart, "Let the world deride or pity. I will glory in His Name!"

PART 1

PAIN AND PRAISE IN A FALLEN WORLD

1

A THEOLOGY OF THORNS

Psalm 90:1, 14–15; Matthew 6:13;
2 Corinthians 12:1, 7–10

*If none of God's saints were poor and
tried, we should not know half so well the
consolations of divine grace. When we find
the wanderer who has not where to lay his
head, who yet can say, "Still will I trust in
the Lord"; when we see the pauper starving
on bread and water, who still glories in
Jesus; when we see the bereaved widow
overwhelmed in affliction, and yet having
faith in Christ, oh! what honour it reflects
on the gospel.*
—*Charles Haddon Spurgeon*[1]

When we read of God's grace, we learn that what God has required, he has provided. We derive from that definition of Augustine's, not only a theology of salvation, but also a theology of the person of God. God is sovereign and God is

1

good. But there are times in our life when the definition of God and our expectations of him clash with
a life-shaking reality. I have witnessed that clash of
faith and life in a young couple when they suffered
the miscarriage of a child. I have held the hands of
dying men in the prime of life, while their wives and
children looked on, waiting for me, somehow, someway
to make sense of God's grace in this. It can happen in
a lab report, in a phone call at 2 a.m., or in the sound
of a gunshot on a school campus. In a split second, the
grace and goodness and even the sovereignty of God
seem splintered into a million pieces. And sometimes
we hear the catchall phrase, "Well, we live in a fallen
world." Our heads believe it, but our hearts want more.
Where is God's grace in such times? How do we make
sense of God's grace in a fallen world?

Our Lord taught us to pray, "Lead us not into temptation, but deliver us from evil" (Matt. 6:13; Luke 11:4).
In this short verse, our prayer is for divine deliverance, recognizing that the entrapment of sin and Satan
would lead us to a great fall. Our prayer is that God
will do whatever it takes to deliver us. That is the force
of this petition in the Lord's Prayer.

I want to focus on one common, but sometimes
misunderstood way in which God delivers us from evil.
It is the way that God delivered Paul. We learn from the
oldest psalm in the Bible that it was this paradoxical
power of God that Moses prayed for as well:

> Lord, you have been our dwelling place
> in all generations.
> . . . .
> Satisfy us in the morning with your steadfast love,
> that we may rejoice and be glad all our days.

2

> Make us glad for as many days as you have afflicted us,
> and for as many years as we have seen evil. (Ps.
> 90:1, 14–15)

I must go on boasting. Though there is nothing to be gained by it, I will go on to visions and revelations of the Lord. . . . So to keep me from becoming conceited because of the surpassing greatness of the revelations, a thorn was given me in the flesh, a messenger of Satan to harass me, to keep me from becoming conceited. Three times I pleaded with the Lord about this, that it should leave me. But he said to me, "My grace is sufficient for you, for my power is made perfect in weakness." Therefore I will boast all the more gladly of my weaknesses, so that the power of Christ may rest upon me. For the sake of Christ, then, I am content with weaknesses, insults, hardships, persecutions, and calamities. For when I am weak, then I am strong. (2 Cor. 12:1, 7–10)

I grew up in the tall, piney woods of Southeastern Louisiana. I was orphaned as a boy, and my Aunt Eva, who adopted me, was a loving woman of God, as well as a good blackberry pie maker. She knew how to get the blackberries she needed without getting all scarred up by the thorns that held those big, fat, tasty berries. How did she do it? She would just tell a bunch of us barefoot boys that whoever got the most blackberries would win the contest and get the biggest piece of pie. She would dispense those big plastic ice-cream buckets and Mark Harrell, Berlin and Ed Coxe, and I would go out to pick blackberries. I ran through the pasture to get to the back, where the blackberry bushes grew wild, wanting to be the first and thus assure my victory.

But, alas, I always lost because I ate most of the berries before I got back. But here is the thing: we had to wear long-sleeved shirts in the summer in order to protect our arms from the big thorns on the blackberry bushes. To get to the best berries, we sometimes had to endure the sharpest thorns.

Similarly, for some of us to be delivered from evil, to get the best berries of life, to grow as Christ wants us to grow in him, we may have to encounter the sharpest of thorns in life.

In fact, 2 Corinthians 12:7–10 is about a thorn. It is the most famous thorn in the history of the world. It afflicted one of the greatest men who ever lived, and it delivered him from evil. Paul had been given the privilege of seeing heaven and then coming back to earth. Paul admitted that what happened to him next was designed to deliver him from pride. Paul was given a thorn. It was an answer to the last petition of the Lord's Prayer.

The Bible here teaches us a theology of thorns. That is, in the Bible we see that we can find God in the thorns of life, in the trials, the afflictions, and yes, even in the unutterable, inconceivable tragedies and injustices of life.

This is taught by Paul as he makes a tremendous admonition out of his own thorny situation. Indeed, the writing of Paul moves to a veritable crescendo that climaxes with this confession: "For when I am weak, then I am strong."

That kind of talk is powerful. It is his life belief. It is something he will stake his life and ministry upon. It is the rock-solid, unmovable faith that transforms his pain to praise.

4

Eight Articles of Our Confession

As the believer looks into 2 Corinthians 12:7–10, he may be comforted. This confession of Paul's can be our confession. There are *eight* confessions we can make about thorns from this text that will change the way we view suffering and affliction in this life. They may even bring us to the place of making sense of God's grace in this fallen world.

Let's look at the articles of this confession, as derived from this passage.

1. Thorns are common to God's people.

We are not told what kind of thorn Paul has. Is it a physical ailment? The Greek doesn't give us an answer. Paul could be using the term "thorn" to describe an issue within his very soul. Or it could be a trouble-maker. There have been at least twelve different explanations for what the thorn could have been. Scholars have made good inquiries, but in the end we are left with the conclusion of Simon Kistemaker: "Whether Paul's afflictions happened to be external or internal, the outcome remains the same: our theories are mere guesses, for we do not know what ailed the Apostle."[2]

That the nature of the thorn is hidden makes it accessible to all of us. His thorn is your thorn, whatever it is. Paul had a thorn, and you have thorns. They are physical. They are mental. They are spiritual. So let us not believe the notion that Christians are people who have it all together and are immune from things like depression and grief. And let us call the idea that physical ailments are punishments from God what they are: lies from hell. Thorns are common to all of us.

Some of the greatest men and women of Christ have been afflicted. Charles Haddon Spurgeon, for most of his adult life, fought what Winston Churchill called "the black dog"—depression. Often it became so severe that his deacons would order him to the south of France, in Mentone, to seek recovery.[3] And it was there that he left this world.

I will give you a more personal example. Years ago I was the pastoral intern to D. James Kennedy. And I will always remember that he lived with pain. His pain at times was so intense that it would keep him bedridden. An elder would be called to lift him out of his bed, so he could go to work in the morning. I am thankful that the thorns in my life are not absent from God, that God is involved with my life and even in my suffering and pain.

2. Thorns are a gift of God to you.

This is what we read: "So to keep me from becoming conceited because of the surpassing greatness of the revelations, a thorn was given me in the flesh."

We don't think of afflictions as gifts. If you are a Christian, God may give you an affliction to lead you out of temptation. The beauty of the gift of suffering and affliction is where it takes you. I once gave my wife the gift of a rose, thorns and all. It was only when it bloomed that the true beauty of the rose could be seen. So it is with the gift of the thorn. Mother Teresa was once asked about how God could allow suffering. This woman, who suffered from a "dark night of the soul" in much of her spiritual life, as we learn from the letters that came out posthumously in the book *Come Be My Light*, said this:

Today, the world is an "open-pit Calvary." Mental and physical suffering is everywhere. Pain and suffering will come into your life, but remember: pain, distress and suffering are only the kiss of Jesus— signs that you have come so close to Him that He can kiss you. Accept them as gifts—all for Jesus. You are really reliving the Passion of Christ; from now on accept Jesus just as He enters into your life. Battered, divided, full of pains and wounds.[4]

We learn of God's deep working in a little Albanian nun—even in his "abandonments," as the Puritans called it—who gave her life away to suffering people.[5] For the things that have come to you to hurt you, in the hands of a loving God, become the things that bring you nearer to Jesus. In this way the thorn saves you, leading you away from temptation and to Jesus.

3. Thorns may be a direct satanic attack against you.
Paul wrote that the gift of God was delivered through a messenger of Satan. The Greek word translated "messenger" here is the word for "angel." This gift was meant for good by God, but meant for evil by Satan. This answers the question: can Satan hurt a believer? The answer is twofold. Yes, the thorn hurts. Otherwise, Paul would not have prayed three times for God to take it away. But the other answer is that the attack of Satan, just like at the cross, cannot finally hurt the believer. Jesus said that we should not fear the one who can destroy the body, but rather we should fear the one who can destroy the soul. Satan cannot touch the soul of a believer, and even his fiery darts, of which Paul speaks in Ephesians 6, if they are not deflected, are redirected to be a blessing. This is what

is meant when Paul writes, "No, in all these things we are more than conquerors through him who loved us" (Rom. 8:37). "All these things" to which he referred were hurtful things like persecution. Through those things, Paul is saying, we become conquerors, not through our accomplishments, but through Christ's provisions in our sufferings.

One of the greatest hymns of the church of Jesus is Martin Luther's "A Mighty Fortress Is Our God." This hymn, based on Psalm 46 and often called "The Battle Hymn of the Reformation," was written at a time when Luther's life was being threatened and he was forced to seek refuge from his enemies. One line powerfully illustrates this teaching that thorns are agents of Satan:

> And though this world, with devils filled,
> Should threaten to undo us,
> We will not fear, for God hath willed
> His truth to triumph through us.
> The prince of darkness grim,
> We tremble not for him;
> His rage we can endure,
> For lo! his doom is sure;
> One little word shall fell him.[6]

Satan's attacks are really against Jesus. We are "in Christ" (a phrase used seventy-five times in the New Testament, almost always by Paul). And so the attacks cannot finally destroy us, no matter how diabolical their intent, sinister their plan, or powerful their blow. This world is not a world of equals. Satan is a defeated foe. His attacks are the last-ditch efforts of a fallen angel destined for eternal defeat and everlasting destruction. "Little children, you are from God and

8

have overcome them, for he who is in you is greater than he who is in the world" (1 John 4:4). So fear not, child of God. The thorn of the devil has been crushed at Calvary by that one little word: Jesus.

4. Thorns can produce a sense of God's abandonment.

I will not dwell on this, but let us admit that the thorn caused Paul to enter into a time of intense prayer. And his prayer was not answered. We are told that he prayed three times for an answer.

I often talk with people who are living between the first and second prayers of life. These are the places where children are still in the struggles of adolescence. These are the places of mothers praying for wayward sons, but there is no response. These are the days when the young father's disease has not been healed.

John of the Cross wrote about this time in his classic book, *The Dark Night of the Soul*.[7] There he admitted the darkness of the time when you cry out to God and you hear nothing. But he also said that in those darkest times he could see the light of Christ the best. The stars seem more brilliant to us when the night is the darkest.

If you are in this place, do not despair. Christ has not left you. His seeming absence is intended to lead you further to his wounded side. He knows the abandonment of God on Calvary, and he will not leave you there. In his light, we shall see light.

And in this place, you are not only being led to God, but, like Paul, led away from pride or from another temptation that could destroy you. Thank God even for the silence. It too has attracted you, if even in mystery and sadness, to seek him all the more.

5. Thorns produce prayer that leads to the voice of Jesus in your life.

At the end of the silence came the voice of Jesus. Jesus' third day in the tomb brought resurrection, and the third prayer for deliverance brought renewed life to Paul. Persistence in prayer brings his voice. And the thorn is the way to him.

I recently visited a dear woman of God, who was going through chemotherapy. Her doctor was my friend, and I was his pastor. He told me, as we strolled through this chemo treatment area, that he often heard stories of God's grace and power in his practice. As he said that, we paused for him to speak to one of his patients. This lady was in her fifties or maybe early sixties, and was receiving what the doctor told me was one of her last required treatments. He introduced us and bragged, with understandable joy and a Christian physician's pride, that she was a model of faith in the midst of her treatments. She looked up from her bed, smiled at me, and said, "Pastor, I tell you, I just bless God for this cancer." I was taken aback. She continued, "You see, preacher, if I had not gotten this cancer, then I would have never met this fine Christian doctor and all of these wonderful people here at his office. But more importantly, I would have missed the joy of Jesus in my life. I have known his love and presence more in this cancer than at any other time in my life. Yes sir, preacher, I bless God for this cancer." What could I say? I just stood and smiled and held the hand of a Christian heroine, as she had heard the voice of grace calling her near, as a result of her thorn.

And what did the voice of grace tell her? What does the voice tell us? That is our sixth confession in the theology of thorns.

6. Thorns lead to a new understanding of God's grace in your life.

My grace is sufficient for you, for my power is made perfect in weakness. (2 Cor. 12:9)

Paul then moves to praise God for this thorn, for it has caused him to be totally dependent on Christ. The weakness caused by his pain becomes the opening for the power of Jesus Christ.

Once I talked to a man named Willie about a thorn that he had. Willie had been in prison most of his adult life. But one day he heard that Jesus died for sinners, loved sinners, and welcomed them. The power of the gospel moved Willie to turn from his sin-filled life of drugs, alcohol, and stealing, that had put him in prison, and Willie was saved. But of course he was still in jail. And he was lonely for Christian fellowship. Well, one of the elders at our church, Colonel Roger Ingvalson, a man who had been held at the infamous "Hanoi Hilton" during the Vietnam War, who knew the loneliness of a prison like few other men I know,[8] arranged to visit Willie. In 1980 Willie was released from prison and was blessed to get a job. Willie became involved with a local church. He loved his pastor. He loved the people. He loved giving his life to building up others in that church. His pastor was smart enough to see that power of love in Willie. He took a chance—kind of like Jesus took a chance, as it were, with his ragtag disciples. The pastor asked Willie to become a deacon. But, Willie thought, how could he, a former convict, do this? Then the pastor asked Willie to be the treasurer. Willie told me, "Can you imagine a thief being in control of the treasury?" But the power of Willie was his background. The power of that deacon was that he was a former convict. The power of that treasurer was that he was once a thief. Jesus gets a lot of glory in Willie's life.

Someone said, "A Christian never falls asleep in the fire or in the water, but grows drowsy in the sunshine."[9] The fire and the water become places where we come to know God's grace in ways that are impossible if we always live in the sunshine.

The thorns that deliver you also cause you to glory in the grace of God in Jesus Christ and bring Jesus much glory and your soul much good.

7. Thorns lead to a new contentment in your life over the other hardships you may face.

Paul moves from confession to contentment, for he says, "Therefore I will boast all the more gladly of my weaknesses, so that the power of Christ may rest upon me. For the sake of Christ, then, I am content with weaknesses, insults, hardships, persecutions, and calamities."

Let's look back on the journey of Paul in this brief testimony. He has moved from visions of heaven to temptation, to pride, to the gift of a thorn albeit from a messenger of Satan that leads to a life of prayer to Christ in his pain to a fresh understanding of grace. And now we see contentment.

When Paul tells Pastor Timothy, "Now there is great gain in godliness with contentment" (1 Tim. 6:6), he is speaking from personal experience of God's grace working contentment out of a thorn.

One of the greatest books ever written on contentment is by the old Puritan master, Jeremiah Burroughs.

He was a member of the Westminster Assembly that produced the Westminster Confession of Faith and Catechisms. He defines contentment in his book *Rare Jewel of Christian Contentment* like this: "Christian contentment is that sweet, inward, quiet, gracious frame of spirit, which freely submits to and delights in God's wise and fatherly disposal in every condition."[10]

And he also taught how it comes: "A Christian comes to contentment, not so much by way of addition, as by way of subtraction. . . . He can bring his desires down to his possessions, and so he attains his contentment." He further says, "A gracious heart is contented by the melting of his will and desires into God's will and desires . . . not by having his own desires satisfied."[11] Oh, that God would work contentment in me! Then the thorn will have delivered me from pride and sin into peace with God.

Finally, let us see the end of this entire thorny journey.

8. Thorns can lead to victory.

Very powerfully and unforgettably, the apostle Paul declares: "For when I am weak, then I am strong."[12] Weakness in the world leads to defeat. Paradoxically, weakness in Christ leads to victory. By weakness, Paul means that the thorn has worked in him dependence upon Christ alone. And in Christ there is always victory.

This is what Moses prayed before God in Psalm 90:14–15: that God would make his people glad for the sufferings they had endured. What a seemingly strange prayer! Yet Moses knew that victory for Israel would come when they embraced the thing that had afflicted them even their own sin and all that came to them from an evil Pharaoh and surrender to a loving Lord.

13

We need to lay our burdens down at that place called Calvary, where God was nailed to a tree outside of a city called holy, and there was sacrificed by the very people he had fashioned in the womb. There, where God's sovereignty and his goodness met, where affliction and passion mingled in the blood of the Savior of the world, is where you are invited to unburden your heart and mind of your troubles.

One of the scenes from my childhood that I could never understand until much later in my life was the scene of poor people singing, "O victory in Jesus, my Savior forever, He sought me and bought me with His redeeming love."[13] I mean, these people seemed to me to be on the losing end! They had few possessions, no education, and little to no hope of ever escaping from the trap of poverty. But they had Jesus Christ. They had the wisdom of God. They had eternal life. And so they lived and died in that simple faith. I have never known stronger people. Though they were weak, yet they were strong.

> He loved me 'ere I knew Him,
> And all my life is due Him,
> He plunged me to victory
> Beneath the cleansing flood.

Conclusion

We must not leave it to a cute little theology of suffering to lead us out of temptation. No. This is hard. Pain is not good in itself. But in the providential hand of a good God, the pain and the thorns are our crosses leading us to new life in Jesus.

14

Each Palm Sunday we remember the happy crowd as they waved palms at Jesus' climatic entrance into Jerusalem. But within a matter of a few painful days, for Jesus, a crown of thorns replaced the waving palms. And nails. But palms and thorns alike led, not only to Calvary and to the grave, but also to the resurrection. And this, too, is the life of the believer: from thorns to grace.

This is now the ruling motif for the follower of Jesus. The things that seek to destroy us, because of the cross of Christ, have become the things that lead us to him. Whatever the affliction is, right now, that has splintered your understanding of God's sovereignty and his goodness, that thing, when surrendered to God at the foot of the cross, becomes the paradoxical power of Christ that turns your pain to praise.

I want to read the testimony of someone who was delivered by a thorn:

> I was raised in a warm, Christian home by loving parents. My sister and I were encouraged to worship and grow at church, and excel in our schoolwork, music, and sports. We were both competitive gymnasts. My mother never fed us fried foods, and we rarely had desserts—and limited sweets. So, at the age of 29—you can imagine the shock we all had when I was diagnosed with diabetes. Even my doctor was surprised when he came back with the news after running the blood tests. After learning that I had the disease, and becoming insulin dependent, I began a two-year period of denial. I talked myself into thinking that the disease wasn't real, that it would go away soon, that there was no way I really had it that bad. My prayers were laced with denial, and I just knew that surely the physicians made an error in my diagnosis.

Finally, God, by his Spirit, opened my eyes through his Word in 2 Corinthians 12 to the reality that it was not going anywhere, the disease that God allowed to enter my body for a purpose that I was yet to grasp. I finally accepted the fact that I had diabetes, and that it was here to stay unless God chose to remove it. It was a part of me. Then, over time, God opened my eyes more through his Word and Spirit to begin to see the blessing through the struggle, and I learned total dependence on him for every need, depending on his strength not my own for the disciplines of this life he gave to me. And most amazingly, I learned to actually thank him for the privilege of sharing in the sufferings of Christ, my sympathetic High Priest. I finally grasped what it meant: that *all things* (good, bad, painful, joyful, struggle, trial, and joy) work together for the *good* for those that are called (I am called) according to his purpose.

I would not have grown in my relationship with him as I have if he had taken away my affliction like I wanted him to so many times. I can honestly look to my Abba, Father, in heaven and say, "Thank you for this thorn." For without it, I wouldn't depend on him for life, walk as closely with him through trial, or relate as well to the suffering of my Lord and Savior for my cleansing and salvation. Thank you for this thorn.[14]

This is the testimony of the director of music at the church where I was pastor before coming to Reformed Theological Seminary. I had always known there was something powerful in her music, but it was a while before I knew that the source of her strength was her weakness. I never knew it was a thorn.

In a similar way of thinking, there is a song that she sometimes sings by Twila Paris:

Thank You for this thorn embedded in my flesh,
I can feel the mystery, my spirit is made fresh.
You are sovereign still and forever wise.
I can see the miracle opening my eyes to a proud heart
    so quick to judge, laying down crosses, and car-
    rying grudges.
The veil has been torn, and I thank You for this thorn.
Thank You for this thorn, fellowship of pain; teaching
    me to know You more, never to complain.
Thank You for this love planted in my side—faithful,
    patient miracle, opening my eyes.
I never thought I'd say it without reservation, but I
    am truly grateful for this piercing revelation
    of a proud heart, so quick to judge, laying
    down crosses and carrying grudges.
The veil has been torn, and I thank You for this thorn.
And if You choose to take it, I will praise You, and
    thank You for the healing in Your name;
    but if it must remain, I thank You for Your
    rod, evidence of Father love for a child of
    God.
I join You in the sorrow so much less than You have
    borne, and I thank You, really I thank You,
    Lord, I thank You, I thank you for this thorn.[15]

Can you say "Thank you for this thorn?" To offer God your weakness is to release the power of Jesus in your life. It is to rob the thorn of its power over you. That thorn may just be the answer to your prayer, "And lead us not into temptation but deliver us from evil." Will you offer your thorn to God as a prayer, so that he returns it as a gift? Here is our assurance: the cross

17

of Jesus, the thorn of crucifixion in Christ, is the gift of eternal life for all who will believe.

Questions for Reflection

1. Have you experienced a season in your life where the grace, goodness, and sovereignty of God seemed to splinter into a million pieces? Have you supported and encouraged someone else who was walking through such a time? What were (or are) the circumstances?

2. None of us has seen heaven as Paul did and returned to tell about it, but what are some other things about which we can become proud today? Are you able to identify at all with his situation— having been given a "thorn" as a defense against pride? Ask God to illumine your thoughts.

3. Name some "thorns" that are common to God's people today. Remember, they can be physical, mental, and/or spiritual. Which of the three categories do you think is the most difficult to endure and why?

4. Does the fact that God sees your situation make it easier or more difficult to endure pain and suffering? Explain your answer.

5. How can something that has come to hurt you be seen as a gift? For what good reason might such a gift be given?

6. Give an example from the Bible of a "fiery dart" from Satan, meant for evil, but redirected by God to be a blessing. Can you give another example— this time from your own life or that of someone you know? If so, stop and thank God.

7. Explain why attacks against believers are actually attacks against Jesus. If you are under attack right now, what is your honest reaction to that truth?

8. Have you experienced what John of the Cross called "the dark night of the soul," where you cry out to God and hear nothing? If so, what effect did the silence have upon you? How might God use such an experience to good purpose in one's life?

9. The lady undergoing chemotherapy said, "I bless God for this cancer." Statements like this can reflect either a belief in the power of positive thinking or a deep, abiding faith in God. What would make the difference?

10. Willie's background as a former convict imbued his service as a deacon and a treasurer with more power than it otherwise would have had. It also resulted in more glory for God. Can you identify a painful situation in your past that could be similarly used by God? If you haven't done so already, would you consider praying about offering it to God for his glory and the good of others?

11. Jeremiah Burroughs said, "Christian contentment is that sweet, inward, quiet, gracious frame of spirit, which freely submits to and delights in God's wise and fatherly disposal in every condition." Does the face of someone you know or have known come to mind as you read that? If you are able, consider telling that one and encouraging him or her in the faith. When you do, ask the secret of his or her contentment.

12. Can weakness be a source of strength? How? Explain the paradox of how weakness in this

world leads to defeat, while weakness in Christ leads to victory.

13. Is there something painful from your past that is still painfully present as you live life today? Are you closer to believing that surrendering the experience to God can turn your pain to praise? Ask God to help you identify what is standing in the way of that surrender.

14. Are you able to honestly thank God for your thorn? If you cannot—but you believe that "what God requires, God provides"—ask him now for the faith to thank him with integrity and assurance.

2

THE LORD OF THE STORM

Mark 6:45–52

*The church is often like a ship at sea, tossed
with tempests, and not comforted: we may
have Christ for us, yet wind and tide against
us; but it is a comfort to Christ's disciples in
a storm, that their Master is in the heavenly
mount, interceding for them.*
—Matthew Henry[1]

Introduction

In between the memories of yesterday's glory and
the promises of tomorrow's dreams are storms. In
yesterday's memories, crowds are gathering, linger-
ing with family and friends on green grass, with
the miracle of multiplied blessings. In tomorrow's
dreams there are still the unknowns. Maybe a new
day is coming when the yoke of oppression is finally
thrown off. Maybe a new time is coming when your

life will finally get to where you've always wanted it to go. Empty nesters with the miracle of parenting and all the memories of child rearing and the dreams of what life will be like for their children behind them are now there, wondering what adventures life may yet hold for them. The young person about to go off to college is there. Summers came and summers went, and childhood turned into adulthood, and now, as Neil Young sang, "It's almost time to live your dreams, my boy."[2] The young man, with a starched white oxford shirt and a new briefcase, on his first day at work, is there. Yesterday's miracles of getting into college, of marching up to get that diploma, of landing the sales job, now seem sweet. The dream of climbing the career ladder seems like a fantastic challenge. The new retiree is there. The miracle of moving through all of the stages of child rearing and of building a career has left you with baskets of joy and even pride. But now, before you, are travel and the pursuit of what you have always really wanted to do with your life.

But always between yesterday's miracles and tomorrow's dreams lie the unpredictable sea and the inevitable storm.

God's Word calls us to see the storm. Maybe the Holy Spirit will name the storm that you are in. But my prayer is that we will see Jesus as the one who was there in yesterday's miracles, who is in tomorrow's dreams, and who is walking on the water of your storm. He is the Lord of the storm. We see him in Mark 6:45–56:

> Immediately he made his disciples get into the boat
> and go before him to the other side, to Bethsaida,
> while he dismissed the crowd. And after he had taken

leave of them, he went up on the mountain to pray. And when evening came, the boat was out on the sea, and he was alone on the land. And he saw that they were making headway painfully, for the wind was against them. And about the fourth watch of the night he came to them, walking on the sea. He meant to pass by them, but when they saw him walking on the sea they thought it was a ghost, and cried out, for they all saw him and were terrified. But immediately he spoke to them and said, "Take heart; it is I. Do not be afraid." And he got into the boat with them, and the wind ceased. And they were utterly astounded, for they did not understand about the loaves, but their hearts were hardened.

When they had crossed over, they came to land at Gennesaret and moored to the shore. And when they got out of the boat, the people immediately recognized him and ran about the whole region and began to bring the sick people on their beds to wherever they heard he was. And wherever he came, in villages, cities, or countryside, they laid the sick in the marketplaces and implored him that they might touch even the fringe of his garment. And as many as touched it were made well.

The Storm

Some people actually like storms. In her book *A Man Called Peter*, Catherine Marshall wrote about one of the idiosyncrasies of her famous husband, who was a Scottish Presbyterian minister: "To step into the living room of our home was like entering a marine museum. Seascapes were everywhere—Peter had seen to that. A huge reproduction of Winslow Homer's 'Nor'easter' hung over the fireplace."[3] He had them in the living room on every wall, in the dining room, in the bedrooms. He allowed no landscape, no still life, only seascapes. He would say, "When you stand before Homer's 'Nor'easter,' do you not thrill to that rolling, majestic, angry sea, so that you can almost feel the cold spray on your face and lick the brine from your lips?"[4]

One of my favorite songs is one by Dan Fogelberg called "The Reach." He writes about life in a New England fishing village. The rhythm of the music and the power of his writing make you feel like you are there with the Maine lobstermen going out into the "reach." The salty, icy sea spray seems to drench you as you hear the music:

> The wind brings a chill
> There's a frost on the sill in the morning
> It creeps through the door
> At the edge of the shore
> Ice is forming
> Soon the northers will bluster and blow
> And the woods will be whitened
> With snowfall
> And the Reach will lie frozen
> For the lost and unchosen to row—
> And the morning will blow away
> As the waves crash and fall
> And the Reach like a siren sings
> As she beckons and calls
> As the coastline recedes from view
> And the seas swell and roll
> I will take from the Reach
> All that she has to teach
> To the depths of my soul.[5]

The early church loved to picture the Christian life as disciples in a boat, with only their heads showing, and with waves crashing against the sides. It was for them a perfect depiction of the Christian life.[6] Were they taking from the reach all that she had to teach to the depth of their souls?

No. They were taking the truth of Scripture and applying it to their lives. In between the miracle of saving faith and the promise of heaven lies the reach in the story of their lives. There we see the stretch of sea, filled so often with storms, and the rowing against the wind as they struggle in the boat.

In our passage we follow Jesus and the disciples from the banks of Galilee with crowds amassing over the miracle of the feeding of the five thousand. The disciples are beginning to see that ministry does not stand still. There is a plan, not fully discernible by the disciples, but Jesus knows it. Beneath the miraculous story of Jesus and his power is a depth that will take a lifetime to understand. With the disciples we also come to see that we are on our way—somewhere. And this Savior is not like we thought him to be. There is no earthly kingdom being built. But there is a plan. To get to the plan we must go to the other side. To get to the other side, we are going to have to go through a storm.

When we say "storm," we mean what the disciples were going through. We mean that place in between the miracles of yesterday and the promises of tomorrow. We mean those seasons of trial and even doubt that come to all of us at one time or another.

Maybe you are in a storm, or maybe you are standing on the hillside launching out and wondering what is out there. Perhaps you have gone through a storm and are in need of reflection and understanding. I pray that Jesus, the Lord of the storm, will speak to you.

Four Truths about the Lord of the Storm

There are four truths revealed in Mark 6:45–52 about the Lord of the storm that, through the power of the Spirit, will lead us to trust him in our storms.

Look at the opening verse: "Immediately he made his disciples get in the boat and go before him to the other side, to Bethsaida." The amazing thing to notice here is that Jesus "made" his disciples get in the boat. Matthew puts it in even bolder terms: "He gave orders to go over to the other side" (Matt. 8:18).

Having served in the US Army Reserves, I know something about orders. Here is an unequivocal command to "get in!" No ifs, ands, or buts! Is this what we expect from Jesus after the feeding of five thousand? Is this what the disciples expected?

Here is the first surprising truth about this passage:

1. The Lord of the storm sends us into the storm to get to the other side (verse 45).

Mark doesn't tell us anything about the order Christ gave, but John does tell us what is omitted here, and that is the reason: "When the people saw the sign that he had done, they said, 'This is indeed the Prophet who is to come into the world!'" (John 6:14).

The people, including the disciples, were in danger of domesticating Jesus—turning him into a local god who would give them what they wanted, rather than recognizing him as the Savior they needed. After all, you now have a Messiah to do just about whatever you

26

need him to do: to overthrow Rome or, for that matter, to deal with your mother-in-law's stomach problems! But this Messiah would not allow these men, who would be his apostles, to shape him into a god of their own making. And he wouldn't allow them to remain the same either. They had to leave where they had been. They had to go to a new place of understanding. And that meant, "Get in the boat. You are going out to sea—alone."

The feeding of the five thousand had indeed brought messianic fever. Many wanted the kingdom to come by force (verse 15). There was no doubt that those on Palm Sunday, soon coming, would want the same. But the waving palms and cries of "Hosanna!" were sung out of tune with the purposes of Christ himself. The feeding of the five thousand was exposing the same inner mistakes. William Lane remarks correctly: "Jesus refused to be the warrior-Messiah of popular expectations."[7] In our passage in Mark 6, this led to Jesus' order and his retreat to prayer.

Just when things seem to be going well, our Lord sends us to the other side, for this is not all there is. Not only were the disciples leaving a mob with a lot of bad ideas about who the Messiah should be, but there were those on the other side who needed Jesus too. The subsequent passage shows us that Christ would bring healing to the sick at Gennesaret.[8]

My family and I, about three times a year, like to watch the classic Andy Griffith movie *No Time for Sergeants*.[9] At the very beginning of the movie we meet this very delicate creature named Sergeant King. His desire is to rest and be quiet and then go off into retirement. He wants no problems, no waves. In fact, Sergeant

Orville C. King tells the recruits that they may have heard that the service life is like the waves of the sea (as he makes wave motions with his hands), but he assures them that the service is more like smooth waters (again using hand motions to show smooth water). Of course, he will soon find that his life is anything but tranquil with those inept and needy recruits!

Sometimes Christians resemble that sergeant. Our greatest desire is for a nice, smooth, tranquil life. Now you can have that if you avoid people, avoid following God across to the other side, and avoid being a disciple of Christ. But following Jesus is to cross the sea of life in obedience. To do that means you will, sometimes, perhaps even oftentimes, sail providentially into storms.

We relish the seasons of life, but we cannot possess them or control them any more than those disciples could hold Jesus down. His love was on the move, and his heart, in obedience to his Father, was leading him to another place. To be a disciple is to follow Jesus obediently from one shore to another.

Now the hopeful part of this journey is given to us in the following verses. Our second truth to consider from this text is that Jesus, the Lord of the storm, does more than send his people into the storms.

2. The Lord of the storm is above the storm and sees us as he is praying (verses 46–48).

> And after he had taken leave of them, he went up on the mountain to pray. And when evening came, the boat was out on the sea, and he was alone on the land. And he saw that they were making headway painfully, for the wind was against them.

28

> And about the fourth watch of the night he came
> to them, walking on the sea. He meant to pass by
> them. (Mark 6:46–48)

The beauty of this passage is manyfold, and we would do well to pause in order to take it all in. There is healing and new life and blessed assurance in this powerful biblical picture.

There are four words that I want to use to describe what we find here related to Jesus being above the storm:

Submission. Jesus at prayer shows his heart resting in the Father's will and guarantees his road to Calvary.

Mark establishes a pattern in the prayer retreats of Christ that reveals his absolute obedience to the will of the Father. Jesus withdrew to a solitary place for prayer after the healing activity in Capernaum (Mark 1:35–39). Jesus withdrew from the excited crowds in this passage after the miracle of the loaves, and did so again before the Last Supper and in the garden of Gethsemane. He is doing his Father's will: going to the cross for our sins, rising again, and ascending to heaven as our High Priest. He will not be stopped by popular demands to be an earthly king.

Intercession. Jesus' prayer while the disciples are at sea shows how our Savior is our High Priest who ever makes intercession for us while we are in the storms of life.

It is nearing Passover in this text. Matthew Henry writes: "It is a comfort to Christ's disciples in a storm, that their Master is in the heavenly mount, interceding for them."[10]

One of the greatest comforts in your life, believer, is that while you are in the storm, Jesus is on the throne. While you are in the throes of chaos, Christ is on the throne of sovereignty. While you are crying out for safety, you have been in the palm of his hand before your first cry. Love him in the storm even more than ever. Seek him in the wind and waves of your crisis, and you will find that he is there. Beyond the sea spray of the crisis is the image of the Lord God Almighty in the flesh, there with you the whole time.

Care. Jesus' watchfulness over us, even as we are in the storm, shows his constant care for us.

This is the Savior who says, "I will never leave you nor forsake you." Can the Lord say that and not mean it? He was watching over the disciples in the sea, and he is watching over you.

> Humble yourselves, therefore, under the mighty hand of God so that at the proper time he may exalt you, casting all your anxieties on him, because he cares for you. (1 Peter 5:6–7)

Mystery. Jesus' timing for our salvation is mysterious but effective.

Please note (in verse 47) that Jesus notices the disciples in the late evening, but doesn't act until after prayer in the fourth watch. That is 3:00 a.m.! Why did he allow them to row against the wind for so long? Why did he allow them to go off course in the storm? Mystery all. I must agree with William Barclay when he writes, "What happened we do not know, and will never know. The story is shrouded in mystery that defies explanation. What we do know is that he came to them and their storm became a calm. With him beside them nothing mattered more."[11] Mystery, yes, but Christ was in the mystery.

Why was it, when Mary and Martha dispatched couriers to get Jesus to come and help their dying brother Lazarus, that "when he heard that Lazarus was ill, he stayed two days longer in the place where he was" (John 11:6)? When Jesus got to the scene, as you know, Lazarus was dead. And so we read in John 11:21, 32:

> Martha said to Jesus, "Lord, if you had been here, my brother would not have died." . . .
>
> When Mary came to where Jesus was and saw him, she fell at his feet, saying to him, "Lord, if you had been here, my brother would not have died."

Christ allowed the death of his friend, knowing that he would raise him from the dead and show his power. He shows us what he is going to do with those who trust in him. In this passage, though we are not told this, it is apparent that Christ is glorified in the storm because, in his perfect timing, he saves the disciples, calms them, and leads them to their destination.

He is like Aslan, the Lion/Christ figure in C. S. Lewis's Narnia Chronicles, who appears from over the sea without warning, but exactly when he is needed: "Aslan was among them, though no one had seen him coming."[12]

I remember watching our son when he was just a toddler during the fellowship times in our church in Kansas. He would scoot across the room away from me. He seemed to enjoy the freedom, but there would come a time when he would look around and make sure he had his mother or me in view. Of course, the truth was that I never lost sight of him. I was watching him even when he wasn't aware of me. I knew he would look around before too long and see me smiling at him. He would feel my embrace as I reached down and picked him up and squeezed him tightly to my heart.

This passage of Scripture tells us that in the mysteries of life Jesus will always be there, breaking through the mystery to become our light. Mystery with Jesus leads to glory for God and good for us. This is what Barclay meant when he wrote these words that I can testify to in my own life:

> It is a simple fact of life, a fact which has been proved by countless men and women in every generation, that when Christ is there the storm becomes a calm, the tumult becomes a peace, what cannot be undone is done, the unbearable becomes bearable, and we pass the breaking point and do not break, To walk with Christ will be for us also the conquest of the storm.[13]

"The conquest of the storm." I need that. I need to know that to walk with Jesus is to walk through mystery, trusting in Christ. That is simply called faith.

Some time ago I came across a wonderful new hymn that I want to share with you:

> Not our choice the wind's direction,
> Unforeseen the calm or gale.
> The great ocean swells before us,
> And our ship seems small and frail.
> Fierce and gleaning is Thy myst'ry
> Drawing us to shores unknown:
> Plunge us on with hope and courage
> 'Til Thy harbor is our home.[14]

Jesus invites you to see who he is and trust that "his harbor is your home." He wants you to see that the winds that seek to destroy you, in the hands of the Lord of the storm, become the winds that bring you home.

Always remember, your Savior sees you. He sees you in your storms. He is watching you in your job that is challenging you to the hilt. Christ is watching you as you are anticipating that operation. He is on the mount, looking into your storm as you take that test. The fatherly eye of Jesus is on you as you struggle with that decision that must be made soon. Though he comes to you in his own time, according to the secret purposes of his own heart, he is there, ascended to the Promised Land, praying for you. "Consequently, he is able to save to the uttermost those who draw near to God through him, since he always lives to make intercession for them" (Heb. 7:25).

The Lord of the storm is above the storm to pray for you, having sent you into the storm to conform you to himself. This truth is before us as well:

3. The Lord of the storm walks on the storm, passing by us, coming to us, commanding our safe passage through it (verses 48–50).

> And about the fourth watch of the night he came to them, walking on the sea. He meant to pass by them, but when they saw him walking on the sea they thought it was a ghost, and cried out, for they all saw him and were terrified. But immediately he spoke to them and said, "Take heart; it is I. Do not be afraid."

The last part of verse 48 says, "He meant to pass them by." Now this was relayed by Peter and written by Mark. For Peter, Jesus was there, the image of God passing by them, showing his love and showing his concern. But they didn't understand the image. They screamed, thinking he was some sort of water spirit. But he said to them, "It is I" or "I am he." Does this sound familiar? Yet "they remain unable to grasp the significance of what they are witnessing."[15]

Is this not the same God who passed by Moses and hid him in the cleft of the rock? He has called himself, "I AM."

Is this not the same God who was the fourth image in the fiery furnace with Shadrach, Meshach, and Abednego? Do you remember that in Daniel 3:23–25?

> And these three men, Shadrach, Meshach, and Abednego, fell bound into the burning fiery furnace.
>
> Then King Nebuchadnezzar was astonished and rose up in haste. He declared to his counselors, "Did we not cast three men bound into the fire?" They answered and said to the king, "True, O king." He answered and said, "But I see four men unbound, walking in the midst of the fire, and they are not hurt; and the appearance of the fourth is like a son of the gods."

And so the saving work of our Savior moved that pagan king to say:

> Blessed be the God of Shadrach, Meshach and Abednego, who has sent his angel and delivered his servants, who trusted in him, and set aside the king's command, and yielded up their bodies rather than serve and worship any god except their own God. Therefore I make a decree: Any people, nation, or language that speaks anything against the God of

Shadrach, Meshach, and Abednego shall be torn limb
from limb, and their houses laid in ruins, for there
is no other god who is able to rescue in this way.
(Daniel 3:28–29)

It is the same God in Isaiah 43:2–3 who tells Israel:

When you pass through the waters, I will be with
you; and through the rivers, they shall not overwhelm
you; when you walk through the fire you shall not
be burned, and the flame shall not consume you.
For I am the LORD your God, the Holy One of Israel,
your Savior.

Do you hear the cadence and the sequence? God's people
are in trouble. His salvation is on the way. His love is
bringing him to us in our peril. He identifies himself: "I
AM the Lord your God." And so Jesus, who is this God of
old, who is the Ancient of Days, is saying to them and to
us: "Do not fear! It is not a ghost! It is not a coincidence!
This is not a fluke! It is I AM here for you."

Some time ago, when I was the pastor at First
Presbyterian Church in Chattanooga, I was studying
Isaiah 43 when my good friend, Dr. Bill Dudley, senior
pastor of Signal Mountain Presbyterian Church, came
with his lovely wife Jakie to speak to our Women in the
Church group at their Valentine luncheon. They told of
how they lost their son in an accident. Bill related how
that tragedy sent him into a storm of sorts: a crisis of
faith, a crisis of understanding. God led him to this
very passage in Isaiah 43: "When you pass through
the waters, I will be with you." Bill and Jakie learned
personally through the loss of their son that Jesus is
Lord of the storm.

Are you in a storm? The good news is: he is passing by. He is there. He will not leave you alone.

Now this leads us to see the fourth truth:

4. The Lord of the storm is the Lord of salvation and is in the boat—calming the storm, bringing peace in the midst of it, guiding us to the other side (verse 51).

> And he got into the boat with them, and the wind ceased. And they were utterly astounded, for they did not understand about the loaves, but their hearts were hardened.

Mark links this back to the feeding of the five thousand. They missed it! They saw a miracle, but did not think that they were really dealing with the true Bread of Life himself! They missed the reality of who he was!

Now you know you want him in your boat. You know you need him in your stormy marriage. You know he can bring smooth sailing to your relationships. You know that Jesus in the boat will bring you the peace you need on the sea of life, and that he alone can direct you to the place he wants you to go. But do you really know who he is? Do you really know that Jesus is the Savior of Abraham, Isaac, and Jacob, the Savior of Paul? Do you really know that you are dealing with the living God here?

Let the doubt turn to astonishment, and, if God is pleased, let that turn to faith-filled wonder. Christ got into the boat with them way back when he was born. Christ got into the boat with humankind way back before the foundation of the earth when, in the face of the fall, in the presence of a rebellion, the beloved

36

Son of the Father said, "Father, not them, but on me let your wrath fall." He got into the boat with us all the way when he was on a cross. He got into the boat all the way when he went to the grave. But he brought peace when he rose from the dead, when he ascended on high, when he took his place as your Mediator, and when he sent his Spirit into your heart and adopted you as his son or daughter.

Now we go through storms of many kinds, but he is there. We are headed to the place, the good land, where he wants us to go.

Will you stop rowing your own boat and let the Master take control? There will not be peace until you do.

Conclusion

I want to end with this thought. Jesus did not rescue the disciples out of the sea. He calmed it so they could continue their voyage. He may not remove you from your sea, but he comes to you to love you, to encourage you, to make the journey with you. He may not remove the thorn, Paul, but in your weakness he is made strong. He may not stop the hand of the Nazis, Dietrich Bonhoeffer, but Jesus comes to you so that you begin to see the shore, even as they put the noose around your neck. He may not deliver you, my sister in Christ, from the miscarriage, but Jesus is with you, calming your troubled seas and assuring you that he has your baby in his arms. He may not stop the divorce, my brother, but he is with you to calm your soul as he leads you home.

A few years back I wrote and recorded a song after I read this passage. I wanted to find reconciliation between the promises of God and the mystery of storms. And so I sang,

> When the wind and waves of life
> Drove my soul to find relief,
> I was guided by the storm
> To find Jesus underneath.
>
> When the storms of life betray
> All the promises You've made,
> I will cling to Calvary's place;
> I will trust Your sovereign grace.
>
> Though Your presence with me goes,
> I seem to still be tossed and turned
> By an unseen enemy
> And I know I need to learn.
>
> When the storms of life betray
> All the promises You've made,
> I will cling to Calvary's place;
> I will trust Your sovereign grace.
>
> And when life is finally o'er
> And I stand before You, Lord,
> I'll see the storms that stirred despair
> Were the winds that blew me there.
>
> When the storms of life betray
> All the promises You've made,
> Let me cling to Calvary's place;
> Let me trust Your Sovereign Grace.[16]

Oh, that we trust him in the storm. The cross tells us that we can. The empty tomb tells us that we can. His presence and power in the lives of countless generations of believers who have trusted him in the storms tell us that we can. For they discovered what we must embrace in our minds and in our hearts: that the winds that seek to wreck your life will be the winds that bring you home, because Jesus Christ is the Lord of your storm.

Now is the day to look through the stinging, salty spray of the storm and see the Lord of the storm walking toward you, with you.

There can be no doubt that this is the Messiah. Jesus Christ is Lord of the storm. He is the Lord of all. Now what remains is the question only you can answer: is he the Lord of your life?

Questions for Reflection

1. Can you name a "storm" from your past, or are you in the midst of one right now, or are you standing on the bank, feeling the wind begin to whip around you?

2. Read the words to Dan Fogelberg's song, "The Reach," and then read the following statement: "In between the miracle of saving faith and the promise of heaven lies the reach." What is "the reach" in the story of your life?

3. What are some ways that we try to "domesticate" God? How does that notion differ from God as he has revealed himself in Scripture? Which do you think would be easier to live with and why?

4. "If we just follow Jesus, we will have a nice, smooth, tranquil life"—true or false? How can you be sure?

39

5. Would God purposely send you into a storm? If so, how does that square with his goodness and promise of care for us?

6. Mark 6:48 says of the disciples, "They were making headway painfully, for the wind was against them." Name some winds that have come against you in life. Were there things that worked for you at the same time? Were you able to make headway?

7. "While you are in the throes of chaos, Christ is on the throne of sovereignty." Is this truth comforting or vexing to you during the storm? Aside from rescue, what could turn vexation to comfort?

8. A careful reading of the Scriptures reveals that Jesus delayed coming to the disciples as they struggled in the storm (Mark 6:47), and to Mary and Martha as they struggled over the loss of their brother Lazarus (John 11:6). Has God ever delayed coming to you in a painful situation? Are you waiting on him? What truth do you find in Mark and John that can comfort you?

9. William Barclay wrote, "When Christ is there the storm becomes a calm, the tumult becomes a peace, what cannot be undone is done, the unbearable becomes bearable, and we pass the breaking point and do not break." Pick one of those statements and give an example of it from your life. If you do not yet have an example, pray that God would intervene and give you one to offer back to him in praise.

10. What is the name that God used to reveal himself to Moses (Ex. 3:14) that was later appropriated by Jesus (John 8:58)? Why is this name of particular comfort during a crisis?

11. Based upon Exodus 33:14–16, what distinguished Moses and the Hebrews from all other people on earth? As a believer, what distinguishes you? How does that which distinguishes you also equip you to face the storm?

12. "The winds that seek to wreck your life will be the winds that bring you home." Where is home for you? (This is not question of geography.)

13. Jesus did not rescue the disciples from the sea, but he calmed it so they could continue their voyage. Are you at sea right now? If so, what are you leaving and where are you headed? What are some practical steps you can take now in order to experience the calming presence of Jesus more readily when you hit turbulent waters?

PART 2

PAIN AND PRAISE IN PERSONAL CRISIS

3

FINDING GOD IN SPIRITUAL DEPRESSION

Psalm 42; Hebrews 4:14–16

The main art in the matter of spiritual living is to know how to handle yourself. You have to take yourself in hand, you have to address yourself, preach to yourself, and question yourself. You must say to your soul: "Why art thou cast down"—what business have you to be disquieted?
—*Martyn Lloyd-Jones*[1]

Introduction to the Passage

Are tears and faith compatible?

I once knew a fine Christian woman, a Sunday school teacher and a leader in our church, who came to my office and told me, "I just can't stop crying. I don't know why. I just can't stop crying."

A Baptist minister came to see me, because I was safe (being a Presbyterian), and he confessed that

45

despite thirty years of ministry, he suffered from a deep woundedness that he couldn't understand. He wondered if he was saved since he hurt so deeply and yet couldn't understand why.

Are tears and faith compatible? One of the most poignant and moving pieces of literature ever written, Psalm 42, helps us as we look for our answer:

> As a deer pants for flowing streams,
>   so pants my soul for you, O God.
> My soul thirsts for God,
>   for the living God.
> When shall I come and appear before God?
> My tears have been my food
>   day and night,
> while they say to me all the day long,
>   "Where is your God?"
> These things I remember,
>   as I pour out my soul:
> how I would go with the throng
>   and lead them in procession to the house of God
> with glad shouts and songs of praise,
>   a multitude keeping festival.
>
> Why are you cast down, O my soul,
>   and why are you in turmoil within me?
> Hope in God; for I shall again praise him,
>   my salvation and my God.
>
> My soul is cast down within me;
>   therefore I remember you
> from the land of Jordan and of Hermon,
>   from Mount Mizar.
> Deep calls to deep
>   at the roar of your waterfalls;

46

all your breakers and your waves
    have gone over me.
By day the LORD commands his steadfast love,
    and at night his song is with me,
    a prayer to the God of my life.
I say to God, my rock:
    "Why have you forgotten me?
Why do I go mourning
    because of the oppression of the enemy?"
As with a deadly wound in my bones,
    my adversaries taunt me,
while they say to me all the day long,
    "Where is your God?"

Why are you cast down, O my soul,
    and why are you in turmoil within me?
Hope in God; for I shall again praise him,
    my salvation and my God.

Hebrews 4:14–16 comments:

Since then we have a great high priest who has passed
through the heavens, Jesus, the Son of God, let us hold
fast our confession. For we do not have a high priest
who is unable to sympathize with our weaknesses,
but one who in every respect has been tempted as
we are, yet without sin. Let us then with confidence
draw near to the throne of grace, that we may receive
mercy and find grace to help in time of need.

Introduction to the Sermon

Living on a mountain can be interesting. Not too
long ago, when my family and I lived on Signal Mountain near Chattanooga, Tennessee, heavy fog would

seemingly appear out of nowhere and descend on the mountain. It was hard enough to see my hand in front of me, much less the road, as I would wind down the mountain in the early morning. It can be a challenge to live and drive in a fog.

Frederick Buechner is a minister and author who loves God. He writes about a time when he lived and ministered in a fog of sorts. According to his story, *Telling Secrets*, the fog rolled in for Buechner when he was a child and his father committed suicide.[2] Similarly, M. Craig Barnes, former senior minister of National Presbyterian Church in Washington, D.C., and most recently senior minister of Shadyside Presbyterian Church in Pittsburgh, and a professor, admits to times of ministering through the fog of questions he has about why his father, a pastor, left home one day and never returned.[3]

A few years ago, John Piper delivered a wonderful series of addresses on Charles Haddon Spurgeon, arguably the greatest preacher since George Whitfield. At the heart of Piper's presentation was the mystery of Spurgeon's frequent descents into the fog, for the great preacher suffered from tremendous depression that would literally debilitate him for long seasons.[4] The hymnist and English poet William Cowper (1731–1800), the colleague of the great John Newton, similarly struggled not only with depression, but also with what we might today label as mental illness.[5]

There is an emotional fog called depression that can descend on the best of us. I mention these three pastors because I want you to know that such times of depression afflict mature Christians, new Christians, and unbelievers alike. Sadly, some Christians try to act like depression doesn't exist, because it is not necessarily the best advertisement for Christianity. Some Christians who believe in the myth of a higher life through good works or perfection in this life fail to account for the reality of this experience. I believe the Bible says it is true. Even Christians are subject to the fog of spiritual depression.

Depression, or melancholia, as it used to be called, is a growing reality in America. One recent study put it simply: "More Americans report being depressed."[6] Martyn Lloyd-Jones, who was a physician before he was a minister, warns pastors to use differential counseling when dealing with this matter.[7] That is, as we counsel, we should differentiate as best we can between problems that are physical and problems that are spiritual. When there is doubt, he suggests that the pastor refer the person to a medical doctor. But when there are signs of spiritual problems, then the pastor should treat them with the Word of God. Lloyd-Jones reminds us that body and soul are linked and play off of one another. I have no interest, training, or credentials on the physical side, but the Word of God compels me to address the reality of spiritual depression.

The Psalms speak to the condition of the human soul. Of the 150 sacred psalms of David and others, there are several genres to be identified: psalms of ascent, psalms of praise, psalms of petition, liturgical psalms, and psalms of lament. Psalms 42 and 43 are psalms of lament and go together. They were written by exiles from the temple. The sacred notes tell us that the Sons of Korah wrote them as a maskil. The Sons of Korah could have been an ancient Levitical musical ensemble, or they could have been descendants of that man who opposed Moses and was swallowed in the earth. Many believe that the Sons of Korah were with David in the north because of the reference to the heights of Herman and were perhaps running from Absalom. John Calvin believed that David wrote Psalm 42 and that the Sons of Korah were simply preserving it as a treasure.[8] Many believe that the word *maskil* means "contemplation," or it could be from a Hebrew word meaning "insights." Calvin, noting its presence in other places, sees this as a particular set of psalms that speak of God's chastening of Israel. These are the hard psalms that teach faithfulness through trial and even spiritual abandonment. Spurgeon well describes a maskil's goal: "It is always edifying to listen to the experience of a thoroughly gracious and much afflicted saint."[9]

So what we have in this sacred text is an insight or contemplation by the psalmist involving spiritual depression. Here we also have divine insights into finding God in such times in our own lives.

The first divine insight is simply this:

The Description of Spiritual Depression (Verses 1–4)

My pastoral training tells me that there are two kinds of spiritual depression, one pathological and one rational. In pathological spiritual depression, there are inexplicable times of sorrow and grief, restlessness and deep heartache, when the soul, for some unknown reasons, cannot be quieted. In these cases there is weeping without understanding.

- Martyn Lloyd-Jones mentions temperament as a possible reason for such cases. Some people may be given to discouragement because that is the way God made them. In this case, I think of Elijah. He was used by God to raise his landlady's child from the dead (1 Kings 17:17–24) and to display the glory of God on Mount Carmel by defeating the priests of Baal (18:20–40). However, these events did not stop Elijah from going into the wilderness. In 1 Kings 19:4 we find him praying that he might die!
- Sometimes even good times can bring about this weeping without understanding. Spurgeon often experienced this after preaching. There is a sort of postpartum depression after victories. We know this to be true in our own lives. These times are inexplicable, but real.

There is also depression in the believer's soul that is caused by real events. These are rational cases:

- Isaiah was heartbroken for his sinful nation. This was a rational reason, an identifiable reason to be depressed. He had come before the throne of the living God (Isaiah 6), but had heard that he would preach and none would respond (6:10). God says in verse 13 that a tenth will return. Therefore Isaiah pants after this tenth. His heart yearns for the salvation of his people.
- Jeremiah wept for his sinful people as they faced certain judgment. His story in Lamentations is a divinely revealed case of spiritual depression.
- The father of the prodigal son had good reason to be depressed. He waited for his son. The

older son continued with life as usual, but love constrained the father. In fact, Jesus shows us that this is the very heart of God.

The Bible says that there is "a time to weep, and a time to laugh; a time to mourn, and a time to dance" (Eccl. 3:4).

Spiritual depression can also come from temptation by the devil. I would say that this is rational depression as well. We think of Job, who was under intense demonic attack designed to break his love for God. Look at the life of Peter, as Satan tempted him. Jesus said that Satan wanted to sift Peter, and he did.

In Ephesians 6:12, Paul says that we are in the middle of spiritual battles, "for we do not wrestle against flesh and blood, but against the rulers, against the authorities, against the cosmic powers over this present darkness, against the spiritual hosts of evil in the heavenly places." This does not mean that we go looking for a demon behind every mood swing in our lives, but neither should we ignore this truth.

There is also spiritual depression when we see our sin for what it really is. In Psalm 51, David confesses his sins and mentions the bones that God has broken. He speaks of experiencing spiritual depression because of his sin.

Sin, it may be said, is at the root of all depression. We live in a sinful, fallen world where we mourn, and the pain around us indents our very souls.

In the psalm before us, we are not given the reason for the author's spiritual depression, but only its effect. It is as if God has said, "It doesn't matter how you have come into this place. I will speak to your condition, no matter what brought you here. I will simply reflect what you feel, without bringing you to the bar to answer further questions as to why you got here."

In Psalm 42, the Holy Spirit reveals a believer who has:

A thirsty soul (verse 1)

> As a deer pants for flowing streams,
>   so pants my soul for you, O God.
> My soul thirsts for God,
>   for the living God.

Longing for the presence of God comes to this psalmist. He uses the deer, flanks hot from the chase, chest heaving and struggling for air, to describe his longing for God. This is a man who knows God. But there is more here than just knowing God. He is longing for the company of God's people. In verse 4, he remembers going with the people of God into the house of God. He recalls worship. He longs for fellowship.

Have you ever been like that? I remember when I was a prodigal son, living far removed from the saints of God and the faith of my childhood. I longed to come home to God. Someone once asked me in my pastorate if I was bothered by the sounds of little children in the worship service. I told them that I love to hear the occasional "Shhh!" I love to see little boys squirming in the seats and little girls whispering. These are the sights and sounds of life in the congregation of the faithful!

Your soul may be thirsty now. Sin may have taken you far from God. Circumstances may be conspiring to keep you away from the fellowship of God's people. This is the experience of spiritual depression.

A questioning soul (verses 2, 9)

> When shall I come and appear before God?
> . . . .
> Why have you forgotten me?
> Why do I go mourning
>   because of the oppression of the enemy?

In verse 2, the psalmist wants to know when he will come before God. He is so far away from the house of the Lord that he doesn't know if he will ever get back. This is the Holy Spirit's revelation of the intense internal struggle of the psalmist.

A weeping soul (verse 3)

The psalmist speaks of his "tears [having been his] food day and night." There are times when we cry like Joseph did in Egypt. We feel we are a long way from home, a long way from where we want to be. Tears are sacraments, revealing the inner places of the heart. Paul says that there are times when we pray with groanings that cannot be put into language.

An accusing voice (verses 3 and 10)

We hear the voice of accusation, "Where is your God?", in verse 3 and again in verse 10. The psalmist himself cries out and asks, "Why have you forsaken me?" Maybe you feel like that. You say, "I must not be a good example of a Christian. Look at my tears and look at my condition!" This was the case with Job's friends who accused him. In Job 18:21, Bildad associates Job's predicament with that of an unbeliever: "Surely such are the dwellings of the unrighteous, such is the place of him who knows not God."

This sounds like a smug Christian who cannot reconcile faith and suffering, or one who cannot trust in God because of a spiritual depression brought on by tragedy. Job replies with all of us, "How long will you torment me and break me in pieces with words?" (19:2). We know that Satan is an accuser of the saints, but sometimes Christians can become unwitting agents of accusation as well.

Remorse (verse 4)

In verse 4, the psalmist remembers the former days of worshipping in the temple. He remembers the joy and praise and a pilgrim feast. The condition of spiritual depression can be seen in this loitering with memories. Those were good memories, but even good things can become painful when they are taken from you. I used to speak with a lady who lost a son in a tragic accident. She spoke of good times, but those memories had now become painful for her. Sometimes we weep for memories of times no longer available to us.

We may be tempted to say that Psalm 42 is a sorrowful psalm. But does it not reflect what we all sometimes feel?

What I want you to remember is that our Lord Jesus was the Man of Sorrows, acquainted with grief (Isa. 53:3), and he identifies with us so well in these times, "for we do not have a high priest who is unable to sympathize with our weaknesses" (Heb. 4:15). Think of his desert experience. Think of Gethsemane. Think of his abandonment on the cross by his Father. You are not far from God when you are in such a low state. One of my favorite places to go as a pastor is Psalm 34:17–19.

This passage speaks to the week in, week out situations that I face as a pastor:

> When the righteous cry for help, the LORD hears
>   and delivers them out of all their troubles.
> The LORD is near to the brokenhearted,
>   and saves the crushed in spirit.
> Many are the afflictions of the righteous,
>   but the Lord delivers him out of them all.

We also have other great insights in Psalm 42.

How God Meets Us in Spiritual Depression (Verses 5–8)

If this psalm simply reflected the condition of believers, we would still be greatly blessed. However, there are more blessings in the fact that this psalm does not stay in the doldrums, but arises like a phoenix out of the ashes and shows us that there is great hope where there is great darkness.

What is the response of the psalmist in this psalm?

Christian soliloquy (verse 5)

The psalmist talks to himself and encourages himself in the Lord, as David does in other places. "And David was greatly distressed, for the people spoke of stoning him, because all the people were bitter in soul, each for his sons and daughters. But David strengthened himself in the LORD his God" (1 Samuel 30:6).

Note how the Christian in spiritual depression is still under the power of the Holy Spirit and questions the forces conspiring against him. Martyn Lloyd-Jones said the great problem is in listening to our emotions rather than speaking to our emotions. This is Christian soliloquy. This is the Christian singing, "Standing on the promises of God." God comes to us as we repeat his promises back to him. This calls for each of us, while it is still day, to saturate our minds and hearts with his truths. Then, when any shade of darkness comes, we shall be well armed for the struggle.

Recognition of the sovereignty of God in suffering (verse 7)

"All your waves and billows have gone over me." Such were the words of Jonah as he prayed deep down in the belly of the whale. All spiritual depression takes place in the lower depths. All spiritual depression is a deep-down-whale-belly place to be. Let's look at that prayer in Jonah 2. Jonah's prayer of deliverance includes:

- Affliction in verse 2: "I called out to the LORD, out of my distress."
- Awareness of God's sovereignty in his affliction in verse 3: "For you cast me into the deep . . . all your waves and your billows passed over me."
- Gospel hope in affliction through a Redeemer in verse 6: "Yet you brought up my life from the pit."
- A time of worship that comes out of affliction in verse 9: "But I with the voice of thanksgiving will sacrifice to you."

The place of sorrow has been sanctified as Jonah, like the psalmist in Psalm 42, cries out to his God. It is true that our place of sorrow, whether explainable or inexplicable, is the place where we must be honest with God about our condition. We must trust in God and his sovereignty, see our Savior walking into the darkness to succor us in our sorrow, and come to praise him through the very darkness that seeks to snuff us out.

This is the faith that sings with hymn writer Margaret Clarkson:

> O Father, You are sovereign, the Lord of human pain,
> Transmuting earthly sorrows to gold of heav'nly gain.
> All evil overruling, as none by Conqu'ror could,
> Your love pursues its purpose—our souls' eternal
> good.[10]

Christian hope in the sovereignty of God for good (verse 8)

"By day the LORD commands his steadfast love, and at night his song is with me, a prayer to the God of my life." This is reminiscent of what we find in Paul's words, "All things work together for the good," and in Joseph's words, "You meant it for evil, but God meant it for good."

In all of this, we need to see that hope in God's sovereignty is a work of the Holy Spirit. This is not moralistic teaching that says, "When you get down, just think happy thoughts." No, this is the God of all comfort coming to you through his Word and applying his Spirit. The gospel in this passage is that Christ himself became the Man of Sorrows, but he is also the New Man and the Resurrected Man. There is a new power at work in the world anticipated by this psalmist and now enjoyed by God's people.

So often I find myself with people or families going through health problems, heartbreaking situations with children, conflicts with spouses, trials from job loss, and with saints experiencing pain from the past that is gripping them and sucking joy from their world.

The gospel in the midst of that darkness is always the same: "Christ is risen." This is why Paul says in 1 Corinthians 13:7, "[Love] bears all things, believes all things, hopes all things, endures all things." This is why Job, in the darkest night of his soul, is able to cry out, "I know that my Redeemer lives!" The ruling motif in the Christian life is resurrection following crucifixion.

Note this final insight from the psalmist:

The Signs of Healing in Spiritual Depression (Verses 8—11)

Briefly, we may trace the signs of healing that the psalmist enjoys.

A renewed love affair with "the God of my life" (verse 8)

The psalmist may experience spiritual depression, but the God of his life is always there. He knows him better than those who have not journeyed away from the temple. His pain has been deep, but as deep as the sorrow has cut, there the grace flows. Through it all we learn to trust in Jesus, and through it all we come to call him "the God of my life."

This man is able to look through the pain and see that God is there with him.

A renewed Christian soliloquy (verses 9–11)

Note that verse 11 is an echo of verse 5: "Hope in God; for I shall again praise him, my salvation and my God."

In his book *When God Interrupts,* Craig Barnes tells the story of how he was trying to prepare a sermon, settle staff conflicts, and basically save the world that week. He had one more thing to do before going home; he had to lead a Communion service at a nursing home. As he says, "It was the last thing I wanted to be doing." He was in the blue funk that sometimes settles over the pastorate. That is when he met Mrs. Lucille Lins. I give you the story from his book:

> Mrs. Lins is almost blind and very hard of hearing. She has gradually become shut off from the world. Her health has slipped away, and now she is confined to a small room, having given up her house years ago. She has outlived her husband and close friends. Very few people in our church still remember her. She has lost almost everything but life itself.[11]

Dr. Barnes wrote that it was a humble scene. He muttered the words, "This is my body broken for you. This is my blood poured out for you." They fumbled their way through, and he guided her shaking hand to the bread and the cup. Then she spilled the juice on his slacks. He thought to himself, "Just one more thing that isn't going right!" He patted her on the back, said a prayer, and was leaving when he heard her so clearly: "Thank you, God, for being so good to me. Thank you that I am not forgotten. Thank you for always loving me." Her simple words were his healing that day.

Her insights are those of this psalmist. In the darkest moments of life, when we are near the end of our life, shaking and maybe even confused, God is there. When we are speechless and deaf to the world, when we may even be spilling our salvation all over ourselves, Christ is just beyond the veil. In Christ, in the presence of the Holy Spirit, in the love of a Father who will never let you go, God is good and God is there.

Conclusion

Dear friends, I can't give you a twelve-step guide to avoiding spiritual depression or a three-point message on getting rid of it, because the Bible doesn't do that. However, there is a one-step guide. It is the step that God took when he left heaven and came to earth. God's Word reflects what we sometimes experience and then guides us to the gospel to tell us that he is there. If he is not, as the psalmist says, "the God of your life," then now would be the right time to call upon him.

Joseph Medlicott Scriven (1819–1886) is not a name known to most of us, though he bequeathed a hymn to the church—an anthem, if you will—for those who suffer in the deepest part of their souls, for those whose tears have become the sacraments of a deep heart longing for God that cannot be fully met until they see Christ face-to-face. This man, Joseph Scriven, was an Irish minister who was set to marry the love of his life. But just before their wedding, his fiancé suddenly died. Grieving, he left Ireland for Canada, to minister there. After a few years of faithful ministry, he met another young lady, and their hearts beat together in a desire for the covenant of marriage. Joseph asked this woman to marry him. She accepted the proposal, and they were on their way to a happy life together. But in a strange, unsearchable providence, this young lady also died.

Alone on the frozen tundra, as it were, of a foreboding Canadian landscape, a battlefield for his soul, this soldier of the cross did what many soldiers do when the artillery fire of the enemy is coming in so heavily. They call for their mother. He longed to see his mother again in Ireland. He longed for home. He longed for comfort. He longed for God. But he took his longings and spoke to himself about God. He said these words, which may be an anthem for all who seek to follow the Lord in the inexplicable circumstances of this life, who sometimes, even through the fog of life, must cling to the promises we preach to others. It is a song we may even sing in the night of our depression, the song that Joseph Scriven left us as he encouraged himself in God:

> What a friend we have in Jesus,
> All our sins and griefs to bear!
> What a privilege to carry
> Ev'rything to God in prayer!
> O what peace we often forfeit,
> O what needless pain we bear,
> All because we do not carry
> Ev'rything to God in prayer.
>
> Have we trials and temptations?
> Is there trouble anywhere?
> We should never be discouraged;
> Take it to the Lord in prayer!
> Can we find a friend so faithful,
> Who will all our sorrows share?
> Jesus knows our ev'ry weakness—
> Take it to the Lord in prayer![12]

He sought God and found him. Finding God in spiritual depression, in the trials of ministry, in the heartbreaking struggles of everyday life, is something we cannot do alone. Jesus, who "knows our every weakness," invites us to draw near to him in prayer. You will find him there, the one who knows your sorrow infinitely better than you could ever imagine. He is there, shining a light of grace and hope and everlasting life. You will find God in spiritual depression, and one day you will worship him through that depression. That depression will become the very thing that leads you to worship. We will bless the rod of affliction as we grip the grace of the King.

Questions for Reflection

1. Have you ever suffered from depression? If so, is it difficult to admit?
2. Does reading about the emotional struggles of some great men of God make any difference in what you believe about depression—or what you believe about yourself?
3. The Scriptures teach that body and soul are linked and play off of one another. Give an example of how a matter of the soul can affect our physical or emotional well-being. Have you had such an experience?
4. Would you agree that it is edifying to listen to the experience of a thoroughly gracious and much-afflicted saint? Describe such a person, if you know one. Might God be using you, or preparing you for such a use, in the life of another?
5. Explain the difference between pathological and rational depression, and give a biblical example of each. Does either one seem more difficult to overcome than the other? Explain.

6. Prolonged struggle sometimes results in depression, but have you ever experienced, or walked with someone who experienced, postpartum depression after a victory? What are some possible explanations?

7. Give a biblical example of a rational depression resulting from temptation by Satan. Do you know of a present-day example?

8. If "sin is at the root of all depression," does that mean it is a sin to suffer from depression? Why or why not?

9. Read Psalm 51 and then the one that David wrote after it, Psalm 32. What does this tell you about how God handles a spirit downcast from seeing one's own sin?

10. How can depression keep you away from the fellowship of God's people? What is the effect?

11. If a sacrament is something considered to be sacred or to have a special significance, can our tears be sacraments? Explain.

12. During a season of depression, have you ever endured the accusation of a Christian who could not reconcile faith and suffering? What was your response then, and would your response be different today?

13. How can the fact that Jesus was the Man of Sorrows, acquainted with grief, help us when we struggle with depression?

14. In Psalm 42:5, David talks to himself and encourages himself in the Lord. What is a practical step you can take—before or after depression hits—to follow in David's footsteps of faith?

15. How does hoping in God's sovereignty differ from simply thinking happy and positive thoughts as

a means of combating depression? How does the biblical concept of hope differ from the secular use of the word as a synonym for *wish*? (See Heb. 11:1.)

16. "The ruling motif in the Christian life is resurrection following crucifixion." How does that truth relate to depression? Does it encourage you and give you hope? Why or why not?

17. The psalmist who experienced spiritual depression was said to have known God "better than those who have not journeyed away from the temple." How can depression become the very thing that leads us to worship?

4

A DOXOLOGY IN THE DARKNESS

Psalm 18:28; Isaiah 42:16; John 17:20–26

*To know that nothing hurts the godly is a
matter of comfort; but to be assured that
all things which fall out shall co-operate for
their good, that their crosses shall be turned
into blessings, that showers of affliction
water the withering root of their grace and
make it flourish more; this may fill their
hearts with joy till they run over.*
—Thomas Watson (c. 1620–1686)[1]

Listening In on the Most Amazing Prayer Ever Prayed

"What people still need to hear more than anything else is that God loves them." I heard John Guest
say these words, and I believe his plain but poignant
insight is unassailably true.[2]

67

In John 17:20–26, we come to see the love of Jesus Christ in the most personal way.

Today I believe that there are those reading these words who desperately desire to know that truth, to have that assurance of God's love, of God's presence, of God's power. There are those who want to trust in Jesus—that he is there in your marriage, in your parenting, in your aging, in your relationships, in the deepest part of your life when no one else is around. You simply need to know that he is there.

He *is* there. That is the testimony of the Bible from beginning to end. Even when it seems like he isn't there, he really is! Sometimes he is there the most when it seems he is mostly not there. When we know that, we begin to sing through the sorrows. We begin to get a glimpse of Christ's glory, and we are led to have our hearts "staggered by the mystery of the ways of God," as James Stewart puts it.[3] I know this without a shadow of a doubt, for the inerrant and infallible Word of God tells us so in Psalm 18:18, in Isaiah 42:16, and in one of the most amazing prayers ever prayed, John 17:20–26.

> They confronted me in the day of my calamity,
>   but the LORD was my support.
> . . . .
> For it is you who light my lamp;
>   the LORD my God lightens my darkness.
>   (Ps. 18:18, 28)

> And I will lead the blind
>   in a way that they do not know,
> in paths that they have not known
>   I will guide them.

I will turn the darkness before them into light,
  the rough places into level ground.
These are the things I do,
  and I do not forsake them. (Isa. 42:16)

I do not ask for these only, but also for those who will believe in me through their word, that they may all be one, just as you, Father, are in me, and I in you, that they also may be in us, so that the world may believe that you have sent me. The glory that you have given me I have given to them, that they may be one even as we are one, I in them and you in me, that they may become perfectly one, so that the world may know that you sent me and loved them even as you loved me. Father, I desire that they also, whom you have given me, may be with me where I am, to see my glory that you have given me because you loved me before the foundation of the world. O righteous Father, even though the world does not know you, I know you, and these know that you have sent me. I made known to them your name, and I will continue to make it known, that the love with which you have loved me may be in them, and I in them. (John 17:20–26)

Clarity or Trust?

The brilliant ethicist John Kavanaugh went to work for three months in the "house of the dying" in Calcutta. He was seeking for answers on how to spend the rest of his life. Mother Teresa was still alive then, carrying the crippled, pouring oil onto the wounds that would never heal, and giving dignity to people called outcasts. John Kavanaugh, on his first day there, went to Mother Teresa. "And what can I do for you?" she asked. Kavanaugh asked for prayer. Mother Teresa asked, "What do you want me to pray for?" The scholar replied, "Pray that I have clarity." She said firmly, "No, I will not do that." Surprised by this abrupt answer from this tiny Albanian nun, John Kavanaugh said, "Why not?" And Mother Teresa told him, "Clarity is the last thing you are clinging to and must let go of." The man said that she seemed to have clarity and understanding in abundance. And he wanted it, too. She laughed and said, "I have never had clarity; what I have always had is trust. So I will pray that you trust God."[4]

"I will pray that you trust God." That is the exhilarating invitation to each of us today in our lives: not to find clarity, but absolute trust in the One who prays for you. There is your answer. There is your hope. There is your today and your tomorrow and your reconciliation for your yesterdays. "Trust," not clarity—not figuring it all out, not getting your answers that you feel you must have, but knowing the One you really need.

How do you get that trust? "Go the Bible," you are going to say. Right you are. But let us go to one particular place, one holy place to find that trust, to experience the deep, deep love of Jesus.[5] Let us go to the High Priestly Prayer of Jesus.

John 17 is called the High Priestly Prayer of Jesus because he prays for his people prior to going to the cross to die for them and atone for their sins.[6] The prayer contains some of the most extraordinary revelation in the entire Bible. Many have tried to plumb what are really the unfathomable depths of meaning in John 17, but all are left with the observation of Alexander Maclaren: "We may well despair of doing justice to the deep thoughts of this prayer, which volumes would not exhaust. Who is worthy to speak or to write about such sacred words?"[7]

I once toured a cavern in Tennessee, and the guide pointed to a stream gurgling eerily through the underground cavern. With her voice echoing through the cavern, she whispered, "This stream runs so deep that only God knows where its origin is!" Well, so too, the word of the Lord in this magnificent passage of John 17 whispers heavenly words that echo in our souls. This prayer of our Lord runs so deep that we can never fully grasp such love, such intimacy with his Father. So understanding—"clarity," if you will—must yield to trust. And trust is another thing altogether.

Jesus' prayer is that you will trust in him. I do not use the word *believe*, though that is the word we use in John 17:20. He prays for those who will believe. But I use the word *trust*. In the Greek New Testament, there is one word used whether our English puts it "believe" or "trust."[8] We have, I think, abused the word *believe*. We live in a culture where "to believe in Jesus" sometimes becomes something different than what it means in the New Testament. There, to believe is to be aware of your powerlessness and helplessness in the face of your sinful condition and the fallen condition of the world. And it is, as theologian Richard Niebuhr puts it, to acknowledge not only the historical person of Jesus, but also his "authority" over all of your life.[9] It is to transfer your trust from anything or anyone else to Jesus Christ alone.

My concern is how you will come to do that. There are probably thousands of reasons that could keep you from accepting his authority over your life. I want you to look at John 17:20–26, for in these verses it is clear that something amazing is at work: Jesus has already taken the first step toward you.

I make my main proposition as clear as I can: you can trust in Jesus, for Jesus has prayed for you to trust in him. He did this in three remarkable ways that we see in this passage.

1. It is remarkable that Jesus prayed for you before you were born.

This is what is meant in this passage when Jesus says, "I pray not only for these but also for those who will believe through their testimony." In other words Jesus was praying for people who had not been born yet!

God said to young Jeremiah: "Before I formed you in the womb I knew you, and before you were born I consecrated you; I appointed you a prophet to the nations" (Jer. 1:5). This accords with what Paul says in his letter to the Ephesians:

> He chose us in him before the foundation of the world, that we should be holy and blameless before him. In love he predestined us for adoption through Jesus Christ, according to the purpose of his will. (Eph. 1:4–5)

Our Savior is praying for his little ones not yet born. Now that might sound funny. Think about this: I do that and you do that. I recall so vividly one time in my pastorate when we had several couples that were all expecting at the same time. I was praying for two families expecting their child through the wonder of adoption. I was also praying for couples that were expecting a child the "other way"! But let us consider, for a moment, the couples waiting on God's choice for them through adoption. They were praying for the child that God had chosen for them before the foundation of the earth. They were praying for safety in birth, for divine guidance in the whole matter of the paperwork through the state, and of course for the day when that baby would be placed in their arms. When that day came, it would not matter what had gone before. All of the waiting, even the pain they had experienced as a couple, was going to evaporate in the presence of love and in the first cry of their new child for food, for touch, and for love. We were all praying for someone not even born.

This is what Jesus was doing. And after this prayer, and after looking over a city that would reject him, he rode into it on the back of a donkey, hearing cries of "Hosanna!" that would become cries of "Crucify him!" Jesus counted it all worth it. He counted it all worth it because he loved his little ones. He loves you.

You can trust our Lord, no matter what your pain may be, no matter what pain you see in the world, because he first loved you. He loved you before you were born. He prayed for you before you were born.

2. It is remarkable that Jesus prayed for you before he died for you.

Jesus prayed this prayer prior to his crucifixion. It is important that you know that you were chosen in Christ before the foundation of the world, and that your Savior called out your name to his Father during his life on earth. Therefore his death is for you. *The NIV Study Bible* note puts it so plainly: "All future believers are included in this prayer."[10] Leon Morris, perhaps one of the greatest expositors of John's gospel, writes: "The prayer marks the end of Jesus' earthly ministry, but it looks forward to the ongoing work that would now be the responsibility first of the immediate disciples and then of those who would later believe through them. Jesus prays for them all."[11]

He prayed for you, trusted in possessing you, and therefore died for you. He did not die and then beg you to believe. He chose you, he prayed for you, and then he died for you. Your salvation is not dependent on your choosing God, but on his choice of you.

> You did not choose me, but I chose you and appointed you that you should go and bear fruit and that your fruit should abide, so that whatever you ask the Father in my name, he may give it to you. (John 15:16)

> No one can come to me unless it is granted him by the Father. (John 6:65)

Now these are amazing words, loaded with mysterious meaning. But rather than theorizing about the mystery, let's look at the practical power of this truth. That Jesus prayed for you before he ever died for you means the end of despair for you who are struggling to find faith, for you who are longing to trust. For you who have been abandoned by family, hurt by friends, brutalized by the rat race, or deeply moved by a world of suffering and pain, this Jesus is already on your side. He does not require that you get your questions answered before he comes to you. He comes to you in the midst of the pain and loves you. You respond when you know that love. Jesus loved you and prayed for you and valued you above his own prerogatives for divinity, above his own sinless life. He was willing to be handed over to evil men, to be ridiculed, to be abandoned by God on the stinking and smoldering landfill called Calvary so that he might save those he loved.

To know this and experience this prayer of Jesus for you will set you free. It will bring happiness to sad hearts of disciples who have forgotten the wonder of his love, for those who are longing to trust Jesus.

Brenning Manning tells of a time when he was speaking at Stanford University in Palo Alto, California. He had addressed the faculty and students about the grace of God in Christ, focusing on the love of Jesus. The next day a distinguished faculty member came to him. He relates what she told him:

> "At one point in my life I had a faith so strong that it shaped the very fiber of each day. I was conscious of God's presence even in stressful situations. The fire of Christ burned inside me." Slowly, though, and almost imperceptibly . . . that fire had gone out. She told how academia and life and stuff just crowded out trusting in Jesus. After a moment she continued, "After you spoke on the love of God last night, I cried for an hour. My life is so empty. . . . I'm like Mary Magdalene in the garden crying, 'Where has my Beloved gone?' I miss God so much that sometimes I feel frantic. I long for the relationship I used to have."[12]

Do you feel like Mary Magdalene when she cried out, "Where has my Beloved gone?" The truth is, he is alive. He did not die and rise again to beg you to accept him. While you were still a sinner, Christ died for you. Before he died for you, he even prayed for you. You can then trust him or trust him again. Your Beloved is here.

3. It is remarkable that Jesus prayed for you, even though today some of you do not want to pray to him.

You may have yet to realize that Jesus Christ has plans for you. What I must make clear to you from this passage is that your unbelief or your lack of trust does not intimidate God, nor will the Father deny Jesus' prayer for you to trust in him because now you are in sin, or are confused, or have troubles of the soul. No, God is like Michelangelo, who saw David in the stone when others only saw a rock.

This whole magnificent chapter is about the grand step that God took toward you before you ever took a step at all. He chose you, he loved you, he prayed for you, he died for you, and he believed in you.

The Swiss theologian Hans Urs von Balthazar states: "We need only to know who and what we really are to break into spontaneous praise and thanksgiving."[13] This is not man-centered narcissism; it is God-induced wonder at an incomparable love.

David was filled with wonder at how God loved him. David, despite his sin and his shame and his failures, exclaimed: "I praise you, for I am fearfully and wonderfully made" (Psalm 139:14). Or as Eugene Peterson paraphrases the verse, "I thank you, High God—you're breathtaking! Body and soul, I am marvelously made! I worship in adoration—what a creation!"[14]

Now let us be clear. The answer to the prayer of Jesus is not related to your intellectual prowess or good breeding to be able to come to him. He trusted in his oath and covenant and blood. He trusted in the design of his heavenly Father, who chose you in love. He knew his mission on earth. On the cross he would be successful because the Spirit would regenerate your dead spiritual heart and cause you to pant for him. Again, this trust is way beyond anything you can imagine. It is rooted in the divine love of God for himself and thus for his creation. That is the force of this great chapter. But when you know that he loves you, it does something. It transforms you. Jesus' trust that you will be his transcends your circumstances, which seek to resist or oppose that love.

The devil in the book of Job says to God, "Sure, old Job is a fine specimen of a godly man now, but just let him lose everything! Then the truth will come out! He is only as good as the blessings. When they go, he will go."[15] But God trusted in his own plan for Job and could thus trust that nothing would separate Job from God. Not even heartache. In the midst of all the hell that Satan could send, after hearing all of the shallow theology of his so-called friends, who told him, "You are in this fix because of your sin," Job shouted out the trust that was born of God's word to him:

> Oh that my words were written!
>   Oh that they were inscribed in a book!
> Oh that with an iron pen and lead
>   they were engraved in the rock forever!
> For I know that my Redeemer lives,
>   and at the last he will stand upon the earth.
> And after my skin has been thus destroyed,
>   yet in my flesh I shall see God,
> whom I shall see for myself,
>   and my eyes shall behold, and not another.
> My heart faints within me! (Job 19:23–27)

I often illustrate what I see in Scripture from my own life because I know that best! I can never forget a little congregation down the road from us who called themselves The Tabernacle. These folks were from many different churches. They had built a small chapel out of pine gathered from the thick woods there in South Louisiana. They would gather on Wednesday nights to sing, preach, and pray. What connected them to my life was that they believed the Lord wanted my father saved. His life at that point was almost at an end, ravaged by alcoholism. I knew they were praying for him because my Aunt Eva and I would walk down a gravel road on summer evenings to go to the service on Wednesday nights. I remember the sawdust in my nose and the mosquitoes on my legs! But I also remember that after the accordions and guitars and piano stopped and we had sung the last verse of "Leaning on the Everlasting Arms," the plumber–lay preacher, Mr. DeValle, would begin to pray. And my father's name went up to the Lord for healing.

Those prayers eventually drew my father into that little rough-hewn tabernacle. And those prayers eventually fulfilled the prayers of Jesus for my father, as one night he agreed to come with us. I shall never forget when he fell down on his knees beside me and pleaded for Christ to forgive him. The little congregation of farmers and gravel pit workers and housewives and barefoot children all gathered around my weeping father, laid hands upon him, and he came to Christ. Within only a few months I would stand and watch the rain fall upon his gray casket. But because of the prayers of that little band of believers, I knew then what I know now: I will see my father again. My father did not pray. He was prayed for. But those prayers led him to his knees and led him to the arms of his Savior. My father had given up on God. But God never gave up on my father.

Similarly, Jesus will not give up on you. He has prayed for you. He did not give up on Saul of Tarsus in his sin. Even when Saul became the apostle Paul, Christians couldn't believe he was the real deal. Jesus never gave up on him. He saw what he would be because he prayed for him.

I don't care if today you are too far gone in the minds of others. You are not too far gone for Jesus if he has prayed for you. The sin of your alcohol may have destroyed your liver and your relationships, but Jesus has prayed for you! He trusts in you when no one else does! Your infidelity may have destroyed your marriage, but God has led you to hear that Jesus has prayed for you, and he will build a life out of the ruins of your sin or someone's sin against you! He believes in his power to save and his certainty to draw you to himself more than you do and more than others do because he loves you and he chose you in love! Maybe you are a child who has the self-image of a loser, of a troublemaker. You may be lost, and your pain and your sin and the devil himself may have trapped you, and you are troublemaker. But Jesus sees a saint being born again out of a sinner.

The prophet Zephaniah wrote: "Behold, at that time I will deal with all your oppressors. And I will save the lame and gather the outcast, and I will change their shame into praise and renown in all the earth" (Zeph. 3:19). Jesus prayed for you, and whatever your shame, it is turned by faith into praise through Christ and his cross.

Conclusion

If you are fearful of trusting or perhaps you feel unable to trust, then this is your day. To listen to Jesus praying for you tells you that he has taken the first step toward you out of his love for you. He prayed that you would hear and believe—before you were born, before he died for you, and, yes, before you even trusted in him. Now you can trust in him, no matter what is facing you.

How do you respond if you are gripped by fear, or trapped in sin or in an addiction, or lost in your pain?

I quote again from Brennan Manning's stirring book about his own experience of Christ in the depths of alcoholism and depression: "To be grateful for an unanswered prayer, to give thanks in a state of interior desolation, to trust in the love of God in the face of the marvels, cruel circumstances, obscenities, and commonplaces of life is to whisper a doxology in the darkness."[16]

David Calhoun, professor of Old Testament at Covenant Theological Seminary, is one of the greatest church historians of our generation. He has struggled with cancer for two decades. In his chapter called "Poems in the Park: My Cancer and God's Grace," Dr. Calhoun relates how he has learned, in his extended time of cancer and treatments and ups and downs, to go to poetry. He sings with his imagination and his spirit, if you will, with others who have sought God in their own trials. The chapters are filled with the poems of Donne, Yeats, Herbert, Cowper, Eliot, Dickinson, and C. S. Lewis. But the poem that touched me was one by Nicholas Wolterstorff. After losing his boy in a mountain-climbing accident, Wolterstorff sought comfort in music. And he wrote, "The music that speaks about our brokenness is not itself broken. Is there no broken music?"[17]

The answer from God's Word is that "there is no broken music. The music that speaks about our brokenness is un-broken." There are doxologies in the darkness all through Scripture, particularly in those psalms called psalms of lament. I have heard intimations of the Psalms, this "un-broken music," this hopeful music, the songs of faithful people. I heard the "un-broken music" in Haitian refugees singing "Great Is Thy Faithfulness" on the first Sunday after a devastating earthquake, as they worshipped outside the crumbled cinder block houses where their own children were perhaps buried in the rubble. This is not human. This kind of thing is something out of this world.

I have seen "doxologies in the darkness" as I sat with a prominent woman in the church who had led a board through a difficult time. She told me of sleepless nights, agony over the trials of betrayal, and the heartache of a trust that was lost. Yet, in tears, she praised God for the hardships that had led her closer to Christ.

As a pastor, I have heard the "broken music" coming from my friend, Ted Mills, as I held his hand and prayed with him as he was rushed into the hospital and told that the pain he was experiencing was a stomach cancer. He told me, "Mike, if this is it, then I am ready to go! I am ready to be with Jesus! But if he wants more of me here, he will heal me. Pray that I can be faithful to praise him and sing his praises and be his

81

witness to all of the staff here." He spoke those words through extraordinary pain.

I remember my friend Rody Davenport, with stage four cancer, being told to go home from the hospital because there was nothing left to do. When he came back into the room from a test, I was waiting for him. I gathered with his wife and daughter-in-law around his bed. He was smiling. He couldn't speak because of a tracheotomy, so he used a voice machine. His first words were "Mike, I am glad you are here. Praise the Lord!" In fact his spirit was so exuberant I thought I was the one with the problem, because I had never been around a happier man! I conducted a little service right there in the hospital, and that room became a sanctuary for our spontaneous worship service. I began singing "Blessed Assurance." As we got to "this is my story, this is my song, praising my Savior all the day long," Rody on his voice machine, mechanically, beautifully, poignantly, weakly, and yet very powerfully started singing too.

"Un-broken music." A "doxology in the darkness."

Why do I tell you these stories? Because they illustrate how God brings us to trust him. He does it, not by our expectations of the Messiah we think we want, but from the far reaches of doubt and despair that lead us to the Savior we need. We believe, not from our positions of strength, but out of weakness. We even cradle our weaknesses—the broken dreams, the unexpected illnesses, the abandonments, and the failures—because in our weakness we see the heart of God. In our weakness in sin, we see a Savior who prayed for us, died for us, and rose again for us. It is in his life, his prayer for us, his loving heart, that we come to know that we can trust him or trust him again.

Whatever you think is keeping you from Jesus is most likely the thing that he is using to bring you to him. You see this is possible because of the deep, deep love of Jesus.

We read in John 17 that he prayed for you. Will you now trust in him that today his prayer is answered once and for all in your life?

Will you pray with me, even now as you are reading these words?

As you pray, I want you to name the pain. I want you to name the sorrow, even if that sorrow is a fear to follow him. I want you to name it before Jesus right now as we pray:

> Lord, I thank you that you are for me and not against me. I thank you that the things that I have named cannot keep you from me or me from you, because you have prayed for me. Lord, I thank you for the cross, where pain gives birth to the heart and plan of God, the resurrection of Jesus. And I ask you, who have prayed for me, to come and open my heart and help me to believe in you, to trust in you like never before, and to follow you like never before. I know you will answer this prayer, for I pray in the name of the one who has prayed for me, even Jesus Christ. Amen.

Questions for Reflection

1. Describe some of the shades of meaning in our culture when someone says, "I believe in Jesus." Read James 2:19 to meet some surprising "believers." How does the New Testament concept of believing in Jesus differ from believing in George Washington or Julius Caesar?

2. How can we know that it is Jesus who takes the first step toward those who do not yet trust him? (See Eph. 1:4–5 and John 17:20.)

3. Have you ever prayed for someone before he or she was born? If so, what was your motivation and what were the circumstances? How was your prayer answered, or are you still waiting on the Lord? What makes waiting on the Lord a very active endeavor?

4. Have you ever lived through a season when you felt an unusual distance between you and God? Was your perception of the distancing sudden or gradual? What were the circumstances? If the gap has now closed, what helped?

5. Michelangelo saw the figure of David in a slab of marble. In Ephesians 2:10, believers are called God's workmanship. As God is fashioning you— even through difficult circumstances—what does he see? (See Rom. 8:29.) Does God ever miss his mark?

6. Does knowing that Jesus prayed for people yet unborn keep you from despairing for others? Does it keep you from despair over your own sin or circumstances? Can anyone be "too far gone"?

7. Brennan Manning wrote, "To be grateful for an unanswered prayer, to give thanks in a state of interior desolation, to trust in the love of God in the face of . . . cruel circumstances . . . is to whisper a doxology in the darkness." What does this mean, and have you had occasion to whisper such a doxology? Are your circumstances such that you could offer one now? What would keep you from doing so?

8. "God brings us to trust him . . . not by our expectations of the Messiah we think we want . . . but from the far reaches of doubt and despair that lead us to the Savior we need." Is there something God may be using to draw you to himself right now? If something is holding you back, can you name it and talk to God about it? (Read John 20:24–29 to see how gently Jesus handled a despairing doubter.)

9. If you do not yet trust Jesus, what is it that is keeping you from him? Is it possible that what you named—even pain or sorrow—is the thing he is using to draw you to himself? Can you explain how that could be?

PART 3

PAIN AND PRAISE IN PHYSICAL CHALLENGES

5

HANNAH'S FAITH

1 Samuel 1:1–20; 2:1–2

S omeone once said, "Never underestimate the influence of one mother committed to the Lord. She is God's secret weapon in the world."

This is a very biblical thought that comes right out of our text. The story of Hannah has a powerful message for every person:

> There was a certain man of Ramathaim-zophim of the hill country of Ephraim whose name was Elkanah the son of Jeroham, son of Elihu, son of Tohu, son of Zuph, an Ephrathite. He had two wives. The name of the one was Hannah, and the name of the other, Peninnah. And Peninnah had children, but Hannah had no children.
>
> Now this man used to go up year by year from his city to worship and to sacrifice to the LORD of hosts at Shiloh, where the two sons of Eli, Hophni and Phinehas, were priests of the LORD. On the day when Elkanah sacrificed, he would give portions to Peninnah his wife and to all her sons and daughters.

But to Hannah he gave a double portion, because he loved her, though the LORD had closed her womb. And her rival used to provoke her grievously to irritate her, because the LORD had closed her womb. So it went on year by year. As often as she went up to the house of the LORD, she used to provoke her. Therefore Hannah wept and would not eat. And Elkanah, her husband, said to her, "Hannah, why do you weep? And why do you not eat? And why is your heart sad? Am I not more to you than ten sons?"

After they had eaten and drunk in Shiloh, Hannah rose. Now Eli the priest was sitting on the seat beside the doorpost of the temple of the LORD. She was deeply distressed and prayed to the LORD and wept bitterly. And she vowed a vow and said, "O LORD of hosts, if you will indeed look on the affliction of your servant and remember me and not forget your servant, but will give to your servant a son, then I will give him to the LORD all the days of his life, and no razor shall touch his head."

As she continued praying before the LORD, Eli observed her mouth. Hannah was speaking in her heart; only her lips moved, and her voice was not heard. Therefore Eli took her to be a drunken woman. And Eli said to her, "How long will you go on being drunk? Put away your wine from you." But Hannah answered, "No, my lord, I am a woman troubled in spirit. I have drunk neither wine nor strong drink, but I have been pouring out my soul before the LORD. Do not regard your servant as a worthless woman, for all along I have been speaking out of my great anxiety and vexation." Then Eli answered, "Go in peace, and the God of Israel grant your petition that you have made to him." And she said, "Let your servant find favor in your eyes." Then the woman went her way and ate, and her face was no longer sad.

They rose early in the morning and worshiped before the LORD; then they went back to their house at Ramah. And Elkanah knew Hannah his wife, and the LORD remembered her. And in due time Hannah conceived and bore a son, and she called his name Samuel, for she said, "I have asked for him from the LORD." (1 Sam. 1:1–20)

And Hannah prayed and said,
"My heart exults in the LORD;
  my strength is exalted in the LORD.
My mouth derides my enemies,
  because I rejoice in your salvation.
There is none holy like the LORD;
  there is none besides you;
  there is no rock like our God." (1 Sam. 2:1–2)

The Lower the History, the Greater the Glory

There are two methods of historiography—the study of history. One involves what historians call "higher history." We are actually all quite familiar with the method of higher history. Higher history seeks to retell history through the "higher" people, places, and events of history. This method is very common and is known by every schoolboy studying the lists of presidents or kings and queens, wars and treaties, elections and assassinations. By such study one may, according to this method, arrive at some understanding of the times. The other method is less known, less observed, but has been championed by such notable figures as Christopher Hill and particularly Nicholas Tyacke. "Lower history" involves the study of localities. This method is like detective work that looks beneath the presenting issues of higher history in order to unlock the mysteries of history by exploring village records, crop yields for particular years, the rise and fall of wool prices, and the lives and deaths of ordinary people. Lower history pieces together the small details of life in order to make sense of the larger events of history.

The Holy Spirit, we may say, is very supportive of lower history. One could even say, "The lower the history, the greater the glory!" Now this is what I mean: When the sordid, cyclical events of Judges end with that most memorable and descriptive line, "Everyone did what was right in his own eyes" (Judg. 21:25), it might appear, if one were only observing redemptive history through the higher historical method, that the covenant of God had failed. Israel the nation was in sin and far from God. How could it be then that the promises of God, going all the way back to Genesis 3:15 and the promise of a Redeemer to crush the head of the Serpent, would ever come true? For wasn't his promise to be fulfilled through God's covenant with his people? Is this not what we saw God doing with Abraham? And yet we see nothing but failure, utter failure in God's nation. We are left to think that because the great leaders of Israel could not sustain faithfulness to God, the promises of God to all mankind were in danger of collapse and failure. The reader closes the book of Judges and is left with these questions, if not with an almost melancholy and pessimistic outlook on it all. It is here, though, that the story changes. It "lowers" the eyes of the faithful reader from Judges to a Moabite woman named Ruth. This woman, this widow, this Gentile, was to become a subplot figure in the plan of God, every bit as important, and even more so than the great judges of Israel. For this woman would show that God's promises would be fulfilled by God himself, not with the help or aid of any leader. Ruth shows us that God can raise up a line, even the grandmother of David and, according to Matthew 1, an ancestor of Jesus our Savior. She is the linchpin of history. She proves that God's word goes forward even when we cannot see it for ourselves. This is the lower history, the glorious history of God in our times. It does not end there. For it is as if God were saying, "I will do this my way. You will see. I will also raise up a young woman—not a man, mind you, but yet again a woman—and she will fulfill the promises of God." The first woman was a Gentile widow. The second woman was a tortured, barren young woman at the point of personal despair. Out of that story of pain we see the prophet who will ordain the king of Israel.

The stories of Ruth and now of Hannah are, of course, nothing but the glorious old story of God's grace—how he brought forth a line from which the Messiah came. The Messiah lived the life required by God's law, and yet he suffered and died as a sacrifice for sinners who broke that law but were loved by God. But the method of observation of this redemptive history shifts from the higher to the lower. It shifts from Judges and national events to otherwise anonymous people living lost causes and broken lives. But they were looking out of their sorrow unto the Lord.

I need this. You need this. For this passage invites each of us to bring our lost causes, our hopeless situations, our broken dreams, to God. In 1 Samuel 1 and 2, we come face-to-face with the great story of a great mother, a great woman of faith: Hannah. Her story begins in pain and ends in praise. The name of this

Levite woman, Hannah, means "grace" in the Hebrew, and her story is indeed a story of God's grace. Here God shows us an ordinary woman with seemingly insurmountable problems who exercised an extraordinary faith. God used her faith to raise up the last great judge of Israel—her boy Samuel.

For a moment, then, let us leave the higher history of presidents and national economic problems and international relations. Let us lay aside all of that for now, and go deep down into the personal lives of each and every one of us. Let us see how God himself brings glory to his name by raising up stories of grace out of stories of pain, how his promises go forward in low places as well as in high places, and how nothing can stop them. He will use a Moabite widow or even a barren girl whose very name may have taunted her for the grace she did not receive. But let us go to her story to find God's story in our lives today.

This story of Hannah's faith is the story of how God uses the small stories of our lives—the lower histories, if you will—to build up his kingdom, and how that brings great glory to his name and great hope to his people.

Let us then look at Hannah's faith in four ways, and come to trust in Hannah's God for our own lives:

1. Hannah's faith is set in her heartache (1 Sam. 1:5–8).

Difficulty and trials are the breeding ground for great things, and Hannah had her share. The story of Hannah's faith begins with her heartache.

A heartache bred by events out of her control

The LORD had closed her womb. (1 Sam. 1:5)

Some wonder if Elkanah married Peninnah because Hannah did not bear him any children. Whatever the situation, one thing was clear—God was going to begin this great story of faith with the story of a woman who did not have any children. Childlessness is heartache. Ask any woman who does not have a child. I remember all too well how painful Mother's Day can be for those without a child. It hurts. In our little country church, the pastor would traditionally ask mothers to stand—the oldest, the youngest, the woman with the most children, and so forth. My Aunt Eva, who had no biological children, would look at me, and I would look at her. Neither of us knew what to do, but she always stood as my mom.

We are not told in the passage why the Lord allowed this to be so with Hannah. But if God is sovereign, there is meaning in our pain. There are some who try to figure out the deep mysteries of life. There are those who want to know where shattered dreams go and spend too many unhappy years of their lives trying to locate those dreams. There are others, like Hannah, who wait on the Lord. Indeed, all Israel was waiting to see what God would do with his people next. Little did anyone suspect that the great God of the covenant would be faithful to his promises by dealing with a childless, waiting woman named Hannah.

A heartache aggravated by an unkind enemy

And her rival used to provoke her grievously to irritate her, because the LORD had closed her womb. (1 Sam. 1:6)

Peninnah was the other wife. God did not endorse the practice of having more than one wife, but Israel sadly began to imitate the pagans, even as people in the church today imitate the world. This family suffered for this disobedience, just as we do when we ignore God's rules for the family. This other woman, Peninnah, was an evil woman who cruelly took advantage of Hannah's sad condition to further hurt her. In the Hebrew, Peninnah means "pearls" and "wealth." Once again, wealth was trying to gain the upper hand over grace.

I know this doesn't look like the breeding ground for great faith, but just hold on! The Holy Spirit is piling on the wretchedness of the condition because faith always shines best when it is placed in front of the black pall of such sadness.

A heartache enlarged by misunderstanding

And why is your heart sad? Am I not more to you than ten sons? (1 Sam. 1:8)

Elkanah, Hannah's husband, is about as deep as the Platte River in Nebraska. The Platte is pretty wide, but you can wade across it. Elkanah thinks, "Honey, you've got me. What else do you want?" I wish Elkanah had not said that, because it reminds every man that we can sometimes be about as deep as Elkanah. There have been times when I have said stupid things like that, too. And there have been times in my own life when someone else's insensitivity has caused me to weep.

I suspect that there are those with Hannah-like conditions reading this—good, God-fearing people who are struggling with heartache. We could go on preparing the soil for Hannah's faith. It is the soil of heartache, indeed. We could point to the fact that the annual feast was probably the Feast of Tabernacles, in which Israel not only celebrated God's care for his people during the desert journey to Canaan,[1] but more especially celebrated, with joy and feasting, God's blessing on the year's crops.[2] On such festive occasions Hannah's deep sorrow, because of her own barrenness, was the more poignant. You can almost hear Hannah's heart whispering, "This is great. Not only do I have to put up with Peninnah and her brood, but everyone is celebrating fertility."

The story begins in heartache, and, for many, the story ends here. But this is not a sad story. This is the setting for a gospel story—a story of redemption. Redemptive stories always begin with heartache. Something or someone must drive us to see our need for a Savior; otherwise, we begin acting more like Peninnah than Hannah.

We see her faith as she endured heartache, but let's look at her faith in another way in this passage:

2. Hannah's faith is sown in her tears (1 Sam. 1:9–10).

This is a real woman. Maybe you have it all together, but the rest of us face challenges with our kids, our parents, our health, our careers, our hopes and dreams, and those haunting things in our lives that won't let go. Maybe you don't shed tears, but the heroine of God's gospel story shed tears. And, of course, Jesus wept. Tears are like sacraments—visible signs of an invisible truth.

The question is, "What do you do with your tears?" We notice one great thing about Hannah's tears: they led her to the house of God. "Hannah rose. Now Eli the priest was sitting on the seat beside the doorpost of the temple of the LORD" (1 Sam. 1:9).

It just so happened that Eli was sitting there. No, it didn't just happen. When you take your tears to church, as Hannah did, you are headed in the right direction. Hannah's heartache became Hannah's tears, and she brought her tears to the tabernacle.

I wish many more people would do that. Church should be a place where people bring their heartaches and their tears. That is one reason the church is here.

I have a good friend, a godly mom, who was grieving over her teenage daughter's bad choices. This friend cared so much for her daughter that she told her, "As long as you live here, you can forget about your privacy! I love you so much that I will not allow you to ruin your life. If that means prying, then by all means, I will pry!" And so she did. One day she found a letter in her daughter's room that troubled her. She went to the high school, picked up her daughter, and told her that they were going to see the pastor. That pastor was my pastor. This woman went into Pastor Bob's office screaming and crying. Pastor Bob told me that it sure got his attention. She cried, "Pastor Bob! You've got to pray! Pray for this girl's soul, right now!" Like Eli, he may have thought that this woman was a little off her rocker, and the daughter probably thought so, too. But this woman was just a woman like Hannah, who took her tears to church. She brought her pain to the right place.

Some reading this right now need to let their heartache become tears and take their tears to church.

Let us look at Hannah's faith in a third way:

3. Hannah's faith is seen in her prayer (1 Sam. 1:11–18).

> O LORD of hosts, if you will indeed look on the affliction
> of your servant and remember me . . . (1 Sam. 1:11)

This woman laid her pain on the altar. The story of God's power is first demonstrated in honest prayers where we confess our condition.

Some of you need to go to the Lord and pray, "O Lord of Hosts, I am in great need! I am not as self-sufficient as I once thought. I am not going to do it my way. I am in need of you!"

A deep, soul-stirring prayer. Hannah's lips were moving, but she wasn't speaking. That is why Eli thought she was drunk. But sometimes our prayers have no words. Sometimes, as Hannah confessed, we can only pour out our souls to the Lord.

A prayer that brought peace. When she prayed and sought God's blessings, the priest told her, "Go in peace, and the God of Israel grant your petition that you have made of him" (1 Sam. 1:17). This woman, who couldn't eat, who was obsessed with bringing her need to God in prayer, finally left it with the Lord in quiet faith.

Matthew Henry commented on this passage to his congregation in England in the 1600s: "Prayer will smooth the countenance; it should do so. None will long remain miserable, who use aright the privilege of going to the mercy seat of a reconciled God in Christ Jesus."[3]

This is my message to you. Don't let broken dreams consume you. Take them to the Lord. You have a Savior who can sympathize. You have a Christ who is seated at God's right hand. Take your burdens to the Lord and leave them there. I want to say to some of you, "Go in peace." You have come with burdens. Now the Lord has heard. Leave it with God. He who heard Hannah's prayer will surely hear yours.

This whole story is about how God advances his kingdom, not through human ways of doing things, but through brokenhearted women like Hannah—and you.

Hannah's heartache, Hannah's tears, and Hannah's prayer lead us to see this fourth feature of her faith:

4. Hannah's faith is sealed in her praise (1 Sam. 2:1–2).

Hannah prayed for a boy. God blessed her with that boy, and she committed Samuel to the Lord. Hannah's first prayer was about her need. Her second prayer doesn't even mention the boy. Her second prayer is really a song of praise.

This is a praise of her heart. "My heart rejoices in the LORD" (2:1a NKJV), she begins. The heart that was once weighed down is now rejoicing in the salvation of the Lord. So, too, the one who mended Hannah's heart mends broken dreams. Jesus Christ promised rivers of life to those who trust in him. I am only one of many who confess that he is true!

This is also a praise that brings laughter. Hannah can't help it. She says, "I smile at my enemies, because I rejoice in Your salvation" (2:1b NKJV). This girl who was named Grace got the best of a bad gal who boasted in having it all. In the end, grace always boasts in God, for grace will always triumph over wealth and human power. God loves to exalt the lowly who trust in him.

This is a praise that exalts God's glory in salvation. In the end, Hannah's praise reveals the core truth of it all. This story is really about the covenant-keeping God. How would Israel be saved from her enemies? By might? By power? No. By one woman whose heartache became tears, who took her tears to church, who turned them into a prayer, and who ended up in praise of the Lord.

Think about this: Ruth with no redeemer, Hannah with no child, a young maiden named Mary cradling the Son of God in her arms as a madman seeks to kill the newborn King, a woman with an issue of blood touching the hem of the Savior's garment, the unimaginable sorrow of an older Mary at the foot of the cross. Then think about yourself with your broken dreams. It really is about God's glory in salvation. For as God broke through to these women and surprised them, and us, with his mysterious and wonderful ways, he will faithfully deliver you.

The Lindas and Bobs of the World

A mother, Linda, in a previous congregation was a very well educated woman and came from the highest levels of society. Her husband, Bob, who was retired by the time I knew him, had been a prominent businessman. They were a driven couple. At their previous residence they were active in church. But they didn't have Hannah's faith—until that unforgettable night, frozen in time, when the telephone rang. The police informed Linda that her oldest son had been in an accident. He died later that night. Their world was understandably shattered. She was soon on the point of suicide. All of the money and all of the prestige offered no consolation to calm the waves of agony that swept over her soul. Linda didn't know to take her pain to church, so God drew her there. The pain that sought to destroy her was used by God to create a longing for understanding, and that longing led her to Jesus Christ. She became a disciple of the Great Physician, Jesus of Nazareth, and she confessed him as God. Then she shared her faith with her husband, who had been living in agony as well. He, too, was transformed by the grace of God in Christ. When I met them, they were the happiest people you could ever imagine. However, their other two children did not know Christ, so Bob and Linda continued to pray for them. I met with their adult children, prayed with them, and asked God to forgive them. They received Jesus Christ as their living Lord and Savior. I will never forget the times I listened as this retired couple shared how their deepest heartaches became prayers for meaning, and those prayers ended with their redemption in Jesus Christ.

That is the real message of this story. It is the story of the Bobs and Lindas all over the earth, all through history. It is my story. It is the gospel story of a God whose love and grace are greater than our heartache and sin and shame, whose power to redeem is greater than the world's attempts to destroy. It is the story of Jesus Christ, the most glorious evidence of a "lower history" of a Messiah who was born to an anonymous girl from Nazareth in a faraway place called Bethlehem, in a feeding trough for animals. That boy, who was revealed to be the very Son of God, lived and died for our sins on the old rugged cross, the emblem of suffering and shame. And all history hinges not on kings and queens or great national events, but on that cross. Your eternal destiny is related to your response to that cross. Christ's life is the glorious power of God in a servant-king. His death brings meaning to our hurts, and his resurrection brings hope to our lives.

You are invited to enter that story yourself, to trust in Jesus Christ for the first time, or recommit to him again, that you may possess a faith in the God who meets us at our deepest point of need and changes us to have a faith like Hannah—and a destiny that is higher than you could ever imagine.

Questions for Reflection

1. Do you have a lost cause, a hopeless situation, or a broken dream to bring to God? If so, describe the cause of your frustrated hope.
2. How are difficulty and trials the breeding ground for great things? Is there such a breeding ground in your life right now, or do you have a before-and-after story to tell to encourage others?
3. "If God is sovereign, there is meaning in our pain." What is the meaning of that glorious truth? Can you give an example through which you learned that truth—from your own life or that of another?
4. Hannah was waiting on the Lord to deliver her from childlessness, but God was waiting to deliver a whole nation through the child he would give her. Does that story of sovereignty make it any easier to praise him *even as you wait* for an

answer to your petition? Since we live in community, what effect might your genuine praise have on the faith of those who are watching and waiting with you?

5. Did Elkanah's attempt at consoling Hannah in her suffering accomplish what he intended? When were Job's three friends most helpful to him in his misery (see Job 2:13)? How can this instruct us today as we come alongside those whose hearts are aching?

6. "Redemptive stories always begin with heartache." Why is this true? Are you, or is someone you love, somewhere on the continuum of a story of redemption right now? Explain.

7. Hannah took her tears to the tabernacle. Where do you take yours? Is your church today a place where your tears are welcome, or do you feel you have to "have it all together" before you go to church?

8. Self-sufficiency and independence are two things we have going for us in America—in fact, they are qualities that are greatly prized and frequently rewarded. But how can these qualities sometimes work against us?

9. Have you ever taken a burden in tears to the altar—either publicly in church or in private prayer at home—and then taken it back before you left? What, if any, effect did this have on the consolation you sought? Are you ready to lay your burden at the foot of the cross and walk away?

10. Peninnah, whose name means "pearls" and "wealth," boasted about having it all to Hannah, whose name means "grace." In what did Hannah

boast in the end (see 1 Sam. 2:1–2)? Is what you are relying upon praiseworthy?

11. Are you able to praise God now in faith before he answers your prayer, before he delivers you from your difficult situation? Why or why not?

12. The agonizing story of Linda (in the conclusion) illustrates how the pain that sought to destroy her was used by God to create a longing for understanding that set off a blessed chain of events. Do you have a similar longing to understand a painful situation in your life? Are you ready to take your questions to Jesus and be taught by him? If not, what is standing in the way? Are others watching, who might follow your footsteps of faith?

6

THE KINDNESS OF GOD TOWARD SINNERS

2 Samuel 9

A Rare Fruit Indeed

A February 21, 2000, *Washington Post* article noted the kindness of Peanuts creator Charles Schulz. Before he died, Shulz provided $1 million to help struggling young cartoonists. This kind man also wanted to preserve the memory of those who fought so valiantly and who led our nation into its greatest years of prosperity. He kindly donated another $1 million to the World War II Memorial Fund. Beyond that, we were reminded of Schulz's great kindness to his family and those close to him.

Now, I do not want to diminish that Christian man's acts of kindness, but I do want to say this sort of benevolence is not that rare. I mean, we have all observed numerous people who have given of their time and money and their very hearts to needy causes that were important to them. One man expresses kindness to his child's soccer team after a losing season. Another shows kindness to his alma mater with a big donation. And yet another person shows kindness to a stranger on the street by buying him a hamburger.

This is kindness, to be sure, but I want to take you to the Word of God to see a rarer form of kindness. In 2 Samuel 9, which contains the story of King David's edict concerning a lame young man named Mephibosheth, we have an exceptional example of kindness. Why did the Holy Spirit record this story? All Scripture is inspired and profitable for us. So as we walk through the days of our lives, I bring you what I believe is one of the answers to this question. God gave this portion of his Word to us so that we might observe the kindness of God himself. This is a tremendous picture of the rare and beautiful kindness of God.

Now consider the features of this rare kindness in 2 Samuel 9.

1. This is a rare kindness because it is a kindness to enemies.

David had won his appointed kingdom, even though Saul had tried to kill him. This passage reveals David setting up the kingdom and consolidating his power. A natural thing for a king to do at such a time was to eliminate all threats to his kingdom. Thus, a king would search the realm to ferret out remaining vestiges of opposition—in particular, heirs of the former antagonistic king. So as we enter chapter 9 and find David in search of members of the house of Saul, we must remember that this act of kindness that David was going to show was abnormal. I am certain that his advisors told him to do otherwise.

Today we have a God who is in search of the lost. This is the force of Jesus' parables about the lost things. He told a story about a lost sheep, a lost coin, and then a lost son (Luke 15). In all three stories Jesus centered on people who would go to great lengths to find the lost thing. Even though they didn't have to, they went looking. There were ninety-nine sheep, but the shepherd left them to go out and find the one that was lost. There were nine coins, but the woman wasn't going to be satisfied until she found the one that was lost. Likewise, but in a more profound and climactic way, a father—even though he still had one faithful son at home—would not rest until his lost boy came home! Jesus is saying that we serve a Father who is restless in his pursuit of his lost children! Down through the ages, God himself is in search of those who will come to him. Jesus said, "But the hour is coming, and now is, when the true worshipers will worship the Father in spirit and truth; for the Father is seeking such to worship Him" (John 4:23 NKJV).

Now this is all the more remarkable when you consider that God is seeking a people for himself who are essentially in a state of war against him! The Bible says:

> As it is written: "There is none righteous, no, not one; there is none who understands; there is none who seeks after God. They have all turned aside; they have together become unprofitable; there is none who does good, no, not one." "Their throat is an open tomb; with their tongues they have practiced deceit"; "The poison of asps is under their lips"; "whose mouth is full of cursing and bitterness." "Their feet are swift to shed blood; destruction and misery are in their ways; and the way of

peace they have not known." "There is no fear of God before their eyes." (Rom. 3:10–18 NKJV)

This is the case of mankind: all are at war with their Creator.

Today you may be resisting the Word of God. The things of God are foreign to you. You have set yourself up against God. You say, "I will not bow down to him. I will not believe in God and in his Son, Jesus Christ. I am my own person, and I don't need the constraints of God." If so, you are a prime candidate to become a child of God! The Bible says, "But God demonstrates His own love toward us, in that while we were still sinners, Christ died for us" (Rom. 5:8 NKJV).

The background of 2 Samuel 9 is that King David is searching for the remnant of a people who sought to kill him, so that he could bless them! That is the background of redemptive history as well: the Lord is in search of people who strung him up on a cross and crucified him that he may bless them with new life and eternal life. Jesus said, "Go out into the highways and hedges, and compel them to come in, that my house may be filled" (Luke 14:23 NKJV). Here is the amazing background to the kindness of God: he is kind towards those who are his enemies, and he is in search of them that he might save them and bless them!

Look at verse 1: "Now David said, 'Is there still anyone who is left of the house of Saul, that I may show him kindness for Jonathan's sake?'" (2 Sam. 9:1 NKJV).

2. This is a rare kindness because it is a covenant kindness.

Indeed, the word *kindness* in the Hebrew means "covenant faithfulness."

David is in search of someone to bless because of a covenant—a sacred pact—made with Jonathan: "Then Jonathan and David made a covenant, because he loved him as his own soul" (1 Sam. 18:3 NKJV).

David, had he looked at this in the world's way, would have sought out the heirs of the former realm and driven them out or, to be safe, put them to death. But David loved Jonathan, the son of King Saul, even though Saul had sought to kill him. Jonathan had been killed in battle along with his brothers, and then Saul himself met his own death. David had an opportunity to consolidate his kingdom, but covenant love with his friend Jonathan drove him in search of an enemy to bless.

Now, the whole of Scripture is based on a covenant. The idea of a sacred promise enacted by God is the binding material that holds the Bible together. Many passages in the Bible form the idea that before the foundation of the world the Father made a covenant with the Son that the Son would receive a gift. It is for this reason that Jesus would say, "All that the Father gives Me will come to Me" (John 6:37 NKJV). It is this covenantal relationship that is revealed in the High Priestly Prayer of John 17. Listen to Jesus' language:

> I have manifested Your name to the men whom You have given Me out of the world. They were Yours, You gave them to Me, and they have kept Your word. (John 17:6 NKJV)

> I pray for them. I do not pray for the world but for those whom You have given Me, for they are Yours. (John 17:9 NKJV)

111

Now I am no longer in the world, but these are in the world, and I come to You. Holy Father, keep through Your name those whom You have given Me, that they may be one as We are. (John 17:11 NKJV)

Father, I desire that they also whom You gave Me may be with Me where I am, that they may behold My glory which You have given Me; for You loved Me before the foundation of the world. O righteous Father! The world has not known You, but I have known You; and these have known that You sent Me. And I have declared to them Your name, and will declare it, that the love with which You loved Me may be in them, and I in them. (John 17:24–26 NKJV)

Here is the covenant love of the Father for the Son.

Just as David, out of love for Jonathan, sought out his natural enemies in order to bless them, so God the Holy Spirit is on the move to seek and save his natural enemies—for the sake of Jesus Christ!

The gift of eternal life is a covenant bequest to those chosen by the Father as a gift to the Son. This is a rare kindness.

Now as the story goes on, David contacted Ziba, a servant in the house of the late King Saul, and inquired about any of Saul's remaining heirs. Ziba told him about Mephibosheth, Jonathan's lame son. David sent the servant to fetch the lame man that he might show him kindness.

3. This is a rare kindness—and it is rare here— because of the condition of the one who received it.

An unmerited kindness. When David came to the servant Ziba, he said, "Is there not still someone of the house of Saul, to whom I may show the kindness of God?" (2 Sam. 9:3 NKJV). The kindness that David was going to express was a divine kindness. It was the kindness that David himself knew. It was God's grace. David knew he didn't deserve to be king. He was just a shepherd boy. But David knew the grace of God, and now he was going to show it to an undeserving fellow.

Mephibosheth did not deserve the kindness of David. First of all, he didn't know David, and had never done anything for him. Second of all, he was part of a camp that had threatened the life of David and the very plan of God. Yet David was searching for him in order to bless him.

This is grace, and it's all of God.

> For by grace you have been saved through faith, and that not of yourselves; it is the gift of God, not of works, lest anyone should boast. (Eph. 2:8–9 NKJV)

We say again that this is all of grace.

A kindness that cannot be repaid. The amazing and touching part of this story is that Mephibosheth is lame. We learn how this happened in 2 Samuel 4:4: "Jonathan son of Saul had a son who was lame in both feet. He was five years old when the news about Saul and Jonathan came from Jezreel. His nurse picked him up and fled, but as she hurried to leave, he fell and became crippled. His name was Mephibosheth" (2 Sam. 4:4 NIV). Mephibosheth would be crippled for the rest of his life, and it all started in the sinful drama revolving around the war of Saul on David.

It is good for us to remember that we are all Mephibosheths. We were maimed by sin from our mother's womb. We are sinners and unable to remedy

113

the situation. Yet we, who have nothing to offer God but our sin, are the objects of a loving Father's kindness.

I once heard of an atheist who told his Christian coworker that he would never believe in God because religion is a crutch. His Christian friend said, "Yes, it is—and I am a cripple." He confessed that he was a sinner. This is the teaching of the Bible. "For all have sinned and fall short of the glory of God" (Rom. 3:23 NIV).

Mephibosheth was a lame man; his condition made him unable to work for David. He couldn't repay David's kindness. But he didn't have to. David showed him love out of his love for Jonathan. And so God shows his love to sinners out of love for Jesus. Now this is not a pagan contractual love, but it is the love of the Father that even sent his Son! God's love shines throughout it all! He is love, he is mercy, and he is compassion.

When God first called me to preach, I was greatly concerned. I looked into the Old Testament and saw the regulations for priests. One of them had to do with lameness. "No man who has any defect may come near: no man who is blind or lame, disfigured or deformed" (Lev. 21:18 NIV).

I noted that a lame priest was not allowed to serve. I looked at my life, and I felt that I was nothing more than a morally lame priest and thus disqualified. I got over that when I realized that all of us are morally lame and that only Jesus is perfect. In Christ alone can we who are lame find wholeness.

I am still a lame man in many spiritual ways, but the Lord is helping me to walk again. If Christianity is just a crutch—as detractors are fond of saying—then I have come to see that I am indeed a cripple, and I need a crutch in order to walk. I have learned through his

114

enduring kindness that Jesus Christ is strong enough to support me, and his steady arm guides me.

Maybe the Lord is inviting you today for the first time to simply rest in his goodness and his kindness. You can't earn it, you don't deserve it, and you will never be able to repay it. You are lame. But he is strong, and he is kind, and his love will set you dancing.

No retelling of the story would be complete without looking at what Mephibosheth received from David:

4. This is a rare kindness because of the abundance of the gift.

Look at this verse: "'Don't be afraid,' David said to him, 'for I will surely show you kindness for the sake of your father Jonathan. I will restore to you all the land that belonged to your grandfather Saul, and you will always eat at my table'" (2 Sam. 9:7 NIV).

Mephibosheth got a relationship: "Do not fear." The lame man was now in fellowship with the king. This is the glory of what Christ has done for all who have turned to him in acceptance of his invitation.

What an abundant gift of the King this is to lame servants such as us! Remember what Paul writes: "For if, by the trespass of the one man, death reigned through that one man, how much more will those who receive God's abundant provision of grace and of the gift of righteousness reign in life through the one man, Jesus Christ" (Rom. 5:17 NIV).

Mephibosheth received restoration: "I will restore to you all the land of Saul your grandfather." What abundant grace is lavished on this lame man! And what

115

abundant grace is given to those of us who have come to Christ! Paradise lost becomes paradise regained! Like a chain smoker who throws away his habit and has his taste buds restored, he again tastes the sweetness of a fresh Florida orange or savors the fresh wholesomeness of a cold glass of milk. The sinner who comes to Christ receives abundant restoration. "All things have become new," and the new believer relishes the simple pleasures and even mysteries of life. The newborn saint basks in the warm golden rays of a grace that is "exceedingly abundant" above all that he could ask or imagine.

There is also an abundance of:

Table privileges at the king's table: "And you shall eat bread at my table continually." As Mephibosheth enjoyed these table privileges, so the believer chosen by God is welcomed to the Table of Christ to feast on the emblems of his salvation. So, he has continual access to the throne of grace in prayer. What abundance is ours in Christ!

Now, as we have seen the qualities of this rare kindness of God, we would be remiss if we did not note what we are shown here:

5. We are told how to receive this gift of kindness.

Mephibosheth received the gift in humility. "He fell on his face and prostrated himself" (2 Sam. 9:6 NKJV). Today, you are hearing God's invitation to rest in him, to accept the righteousness of Jesus Christ, and to bask in his unconditional love. The true believer doesn't boast in his faith, but recognizes it for what it is: a gift of God.

Mephibosheth received the gift with his family. Not only did Mephibosheth receive this gift, but so also did his young son Micha (2 Sam. 9:12). Now, Micha could rise up and rebel against the gift or receive it as his own inheritance.

Such is the case with you and your family. If you have trusted in Jesus, God extends that covenant love to your children. It's not salvation by association, but the blessing of the knowledge of the gospel by association. "Train up a child in the way he should go: and when he is old he will not depart from it" (Prov. 22:6 NKJV).

We know we are saved by faith alone in Christ, but isn't it a blessing to get a head start—as it were—by being a member of a family that has received the blessing of salvation? Pass this faith on to your children and bring them to the house of God to worship King Jesus. He bids them to come and partake of the blessings he has bestowed upon you.

Conclusion

Look at the end of the story. It started with a kind-hearted king in search of an enemy to bless. It ends with a transformed man sitting at David's table: "And Mephibosheth lived in Jerusalem, because he always ate at the king's table." The story ends with these words, as if to accent the amazing thing about it all: "And he was crippled in both feet" (2 Sam. 9:13 NIV).

What a picture. Think about this: anyone coming into the house of David and observing his royal table wouldn't know about Mephibosheth's past. His legs might have been hidden under the table. Or, for as much as any observer knew, this man was just another family member eating with the king.

You too will see Mephibosheths all over the church! They are the changed lives of those who sing to God's glory like freed songbirds! You see them preaching the Word of God like ambassadors of heaven itself! You find them there at the house of the Lord, happily teaching and ushering and singing the hymns of the church.

But we know that at the table, under the blessings, behind the songs and the sermons and the happy hymns, are lame men and women. You see, believers are no different than lame men and women who are not followers of Jesus Christ—except for this: they have heard the invitation, have come into the King's house, and are dining on heavenly fare—even though they're just a bunch of recovering sinners.

Have you accepted the invitation of a kind Savior who bids you to come—just the way you are? Don't let your lameness hold you back. His kindness will set you to dancing.

Questions for Reflection

1. God seeks worshippers (John 4:23), and Jesus came to seek and to save that which was lost (Luke 19:10). How are these two truths intimately related?
2. If the eye has an inner fitness for seeing, and the ear has an inner fitness for hearing, what is your inner fitness for worshipping God in spirit and truth? Were you born with this inner fitness? If not, how did you become fit to worship God?
3. How is one considered an enemy of God (Rom. 3:10–18)? How is one considered a friend of

God (John 15:13–17)? Is there any other category? Why or why not?

4. In the Hebrew of the Old Testament, kindness means "covenant faithfulness," and a covenant is a sacred promise enacted by God. What is it that God "promised" Jesus (see John 17:6–11)? How does King David's covenant promise to Jonathan foreshadow this (2 Sam. 9:3)?

5. If justice is getting what you deserve, and mercy is not getting what you deserve, how would you describe grace? What made David's kindness to Mephibosheth gracious?

6. Do you have anything in common with Mephibosheth? What does David's kindness to him have in common with God's kindness to you?

7. Mephibosheth was granted a special relationship with the king, restoration of his grandfather's lands and the privilege of dining with the king (2 Sam. 9:7). Compare theses three gracious grants to the privileges enjoyed by those who belong to Christ.

8. Mephibosheth's son Micha also received the gracious grants. Does this mean the children of Christians are saved by virtue of the faith of their parents? Why or why not? Is any advantage extended to the children of believers?

9. Mephibosheth's crippled legs were hidden under the king's table as he dined there. Likewise, the things that cripple us in life are often hidden from others. Is there something—known only to you—that is preventing you from running to Jesus? Read Luke 15:11–20. Who does the running in this story of grace?

PART 4

PAIN AND PRAISE IN PAINFUL MEMORIES

7

THE GRACE OF LOCUST SHELLS, OR HOW GOD REDEEMS THE PAIN OF OUR PAST

Joel 2:24–27; 1 Corinthians 1:30; 15:1–10;
2 Corinthians 5:17

He that is down need fear no fall,
He that is low no pride.
He that is humble ever shall
Have God to be his guide.
—John Bunyan[1]

Gathering Locusts

There is a song called "In the Land of Beginning Again" that Bing Crosby sang in the movie *The Bells of St. Mary's.* It begins:

There's a land of beginning again
Where skies are always blue

Though we've made mistakes, that's true
Let's forget the past and start life anew
Though we wander by a river of tears
Where sunshine won't come through
Let's find that paradise where sorrow can't live
And learn the teachings of forget and forgive
In the land of beginning again
Where broken dreams come true.[2]

Is it mere Hollywood sentiment to think that there is such a place in this life? We all want to go to the land of beginning again, for we all make mistakes. But how do we get there? Journey with me back nearly three millennia to a time when a prophet named Joel ministered to a broken people, and you will see that the land of beginning again is actually a place promised to us in the Bible.

Was this message to us written before or after the exile? There are hints that it was written before, but others see it having been written later. John Calvin was right in saying that we just don't know.[3] I have learned that the Holy Spirit often conceals things, not to create mystery that is out of reach, but to draw us in to say, "This is for you! This is for every age!" I believe that is so in the book of Joel.

At the center of the story are locusts. Somewhere in Israel a child comes upon a locust shell, empty and crusty, and asks, "Dad, what is this?"

The answer to that question leads to our healing. The answer comes from selections in Joel, the gospel of Mark, and 1 and 2 Corinthians.

Here is the inerrant and infallible Word of God:

The threshing floors shall be full of grain;
    the vats shall overflow with wine and oil.

I will restore to you the years
    that the swarming locust has eaten,
the hopper, the destroyer, and the cutter,
    my great army, which I sent among you.

You shall eat in plenty and be satisfied,
    and praise the name of the LORD your God,
    who has dealt wondrously with you.
And my people shall never again be put to shame.
You shall know that I am in the midst of Israel,
    and that I am the LORD your God and there is
        none else.
And my people shall never again be put to shame.
    (Joel 2:24–27)

They came to the other side of the sea, to the country of the [Gadarenes]. And when Jesus had stepped out of the boat, immediately there met him out of the tombs a man with an unclean spirit. He lived among the tombs. And no one could bind him anymore, not even with a chain, for he had often been bound with shackles and chains, but he wrenched the chains apart, and he broke the shackles in pieces. No one had the strength to subdue him. Night and day among the tombs and on the mountains he was always crying out and cutting himself with stones. And when he saw Jesus from afar, he ran and fell down before him. And crying out with a loud voice, he said, "What have you to do with me, Jesus, Son of the Most High God? I adjure you by God, do not torment me." For he was saying to him, "Come out of the man, you unclean spirit!" And Jesus asked him, "What is your name?" He replied, "My name is Legion, for we are many." And he begged him earnestly not to send them out of the country. Now a great herd of pigs was feeding there on the hillside, and they begged him, saying,

"Send us to the pigs; let us enter them." So he gave them permission. And the unclean spirits came out, and entered the pigs, and the herd, numbering about two thousand, rushed down the steep bank into the sea and were drowned in the sea. (Mark 5:1–13)

As he was getting into the boat, the man who had been possessed with demons begged him that he might be with him. And he did not permit him but said to him, "Go home to your friends and tell them how much the Lord has done for you, and how he has had mercy on you." And he went away and began to proclaim in the Decapolis how much Jesus had done for him, and everyone marveled. (Mark 5:18–20)

And because of him you are in Christ Jesus, who became to us wisdom from God, righteousness and sanctification and redemption. (1 Cor. 1:30)

Now I would remind you, brothers, of the gospel I preached to you, which you received, in which you stand, and by which you are being saved, if you hold fast to the word I preached to you—unless you believed in vain. For I delivered to you as of first importance what I also received: that Christ died for our sins in accordance with the Scriptures, that he was buried, that he was raised on the third day in accordance with the Scriptures, and that he appeared to Cephas, then to the twelve. Then he appeared to more than five hundred brothers at one time, most of whom are still alive, though some have fallen asleep. Then he appeared to James, then to all the apostles. Last of all, as to one untimely born, he appeared also to me. For I am the least of the apostles, unworthy to be called an apostle, because I persecuted the church of God. But by the grace of

God I am what I am, and his grace toward me was not in vain. On the contrary, I worked harder than any of them, though it was not I, but the grace of God that is with me. (1 Cor. 15:1–10)

Therefore, if anyone is in Christ, he is a new creation. The old has passed away; behold, the new has come. (2 Cor. 5:17)

Cicada Shells for Aunt Eva

When I was a child, I used to gather locust shells and bring them to Aunt Eva as a present. Now when I say locust, I really mean cicada. The cicada, after mating in the spring, scratches a little burrow in a tree and buries her eggs there. Then she goes off to die. Between June and October each of the 18 million living descendants grows and feeds off the tree, eating into its roots. The survivors climb up the tree that they have been eating, and then through the miracle of metamorphosis they emerge as new creatures, leaving their old shells behind on the tree. Well, I used to gather these locust shells, as many as fifty or more at a time, and bring them as a childish gift to my sweetheart, my Aunt Eva. She would gather up her apron and receive the crusty remains and smile with approval. And I wonder, these many years later, what she thought of that gift: the shells of locusts that ate our trees, a minor plague on her Crape Myrtles, all laid before her as a gift of my love.

The Bible talks a lot about locusts as creatures that symbolize the destruction of the land that gives crops and thus life. This verse about locusts has become very important in my life: "I will restore to you the years that the swarming locust has eaten, the hopper, the

127

destroyer, and the cutter, my great army, which I sent among you" (Joel 2:25).[4]

Now I admit that this verse will never make it on a sign in a nationally televised football game, like John 3:16, but for me it is every bit as meaningful. When I sign books for people, this is a verse that I often use under my name, hoping that they will say, "Wow, that is weird. I have never seen that one. I think I will look it up in the Bible to see what it says!" I pray that God will inscribe Joel 2:25 on your soul forevermore. I might wish that you would devour the passage, for some people eat locusts. You may never want to eat a locust, but you will definitely want to have this biblical delicacy in your life.

The reason this verse is so powerful is that it teaches that God will heal the pain of our past and give us a new life. The way that he does that is a miracle. There are places for therapy. There is a need for medication. But miracles can happen to heal the broken heart and bind up the wounds of life, and give you everlasting life.

First I need to say three things about this little book of Joel that will help us better understand the power of this passage.

Three Great Things to Know About the Book of Joel

1. The land looms large in Joel (1:1–4).

In Hebrew the word for "the land" is *ha'arets*. A theology of the land in Joel shows us that this is more than just dirt and gravel, shoreline, and mountain and valley. It is more than real estate. *Ha'arets* in Joel is the place where life is lived. *Ha'arets* in the Bible is always the place where we were meant to be. Much of Genesis is about the land: the garden of Eden, the loss of that land, the promise of land, the journey to that land by a man named Abraham. And in Exodus God brings the sojourning Hebrew slaves out of Egypt so that they may possess the land. In Joshua they fight for the land. They win and possess it, only to lose it through sin. When the prophets warn the Israelites about their sin, they warn them of a loss of land and of exile in a foreign land. But God promises restoration. And after seventy years many exiles return to the land.

In the New Testament the promised land is a new Jerusalem.[5] Christians are on a journey to a better country, the book of Hebrews tells us. But always, throughout the whole of the Bible, we are to return to a place, an Eden, a land.

We read in Joel 1:1–4:

The word of the LORD that came to Joel, the son of Pethuel:

Hear this, you elders;
    give ear, all inhabitants of the land!
Has such a thing happened in your days,
    or in the days of your fathers?
Tell your children of it,
    and let your children tell their children,
    and their children to another generation.

What the cutting locust left,
    the swarming locust has eaten.
What the swarming locust left,
    the hopping locust has eaten,
and what the hopping locust left,
    the destroying locust has eaten.

Every kind of locust imaginable has totally destroyed the land. They are described as being so horribly devastating that no one has ever seen anything like it:

> Has such a thing happened in your days,
>> or in the days of your fathers? (1:2)

> Their like has never been before, nor will it be again
>> after them. (2:2)

This is something to tell your children, and for them to tell their children, and for their children to tell another generation (1:3). Nothing is left. All is gone. Life, supported by the land, cannot be sustained without divine intervention. The judgment is impacting the land, the farmers, the priests, everything.[6]

But there is more. The locusts, once sent upon an unyielding Pharaoh, and now sent on Judah, the southern kingdom, portends a greater power that shall come. For we read in verses 6–7:

> For a nation has come up against my land,
>> powerful and beyond number;
> its teeth are lion's teeth,
>> and it has the fangs of a lioness.
> It has laid waste my vine
>> and splintered my fig tree;
> it has stripped off their bark and thrown it down;
>> their branches are made white.

The enemies of God's people, Tyre and Sidon, Egypt and Edom, and the northern enemy, all mentioned in Joel, are exactly like the locust. Indeed, these enemies and God's dealing with them look into the future to the day of the Lord. The land is laid waste, but God will move across the land and renew it.

The rest of Joel is about the renewal of the people's heart, and God's restoration of the land to them and to all who will turn to him.[7] Do you know what this means for you? The book of Joel teaches us that God saves us, body and soul. He is concerned about saving your soul, as well as giving you a home, a future, and a hope in him. He is concerned about your family, your work, your health, your education, your goals, and your thought life. He has provided a way for you to know peace in all of these areas, through his Son Jesus Christ and through his instruction by his Spirit in us.

So that is the first thing: the land looms large. The second thing you must know about Joel is this:

2. The Lord stands sovereign in Joel (2:25).

In Joel there is no mystery in how the locust came to destroy the land. The Lord speaks of "my great army, which I sent among you." And there is no mystery in how the land will recover: "I will restore to you the years" (2:25).

The answer throughout Joel—throughout the Bible and throughout your life—is hard to take sometimes, but it is undeniable. The answer is God. He is the answer to the mystery, if you will—the figure of one walking on the water of the storm. His sovereignty may be plainly revealed, but incomprehensible to the heart. We read of his sovereignty in all things, but we cannot figure it out. God, who is without sin, ordained and orchestrated the destruction. That is the mystery. I once chafed at the clear teaching of this doctrine. But as I bowed to this God of all power, I found I could sing these beautiful words of the great Canadian hymn writer, Margaret Clarkson:

> O Father, You are sovereign, the Lord of human pain,
> Transmuting earthly sorrows to gold of heav'nly gain.
> All evil overruling, as none by Conqu'ror could,
> Your love pursues its purpose—our souls' eternal good.[8]

The Egyptians who enslaved Israel were tools. The Edomites who terrorized the city of God were instruments. And they would have to bear the burden of their sin, their violation of God's people. But God says that he is the one who sent the locust. He is also the one who restored his people. Accepting God's sovereignty in judgment, as uncomfortable as that may be for us, is to accept his sovereignty in salvation and renewal. For this is the God who says,

> Fear not, O land;
>   be glad and rejoice,
>   for the Lord has done great things!
> Fear not, you beasts of the field,
>   for the pastures of the wilderness are green;
> . . . .
> "Be glad, O children of Zion,
>   and rejoice in the Lord your God,
> for he has given the early rain for your vindication;
>   he has poured down for you abundant rain,
>   the early and the latter rain, as before.
> . . . .
> I will restore to you the years that the . . . locust has
>   eaten. (Joel 2:21–23, 25)

132

Look at 2:26:

> You shall eat in plenty and be satisfied,
>   and praise the name of the Lord your God,
>   who has dealt wondrously with you.
> And my people shall never again be put to shame."

What grace! All life affected by God's judgment on man's sin will now enjoy renewal! The land, the beasts, and of course God's own people. Gladness. Green meadows. New years of fruitfulness. No more shame. And why? Because of the sovereign grace of God. As one commentator puts it, "The steadfast love and compassion of our Father God drives Him in all His dealings with His people."[9]

I think of Churchill's "Finest Hour" speech to Britain, as he held out hope of a new day, once the locusts of Nazi oppression were destroyed, when he spoke about "broad, sunlit uplands" of new life.[10]

The hand of God brought all of this about. Sin led to his devastating judgment. Repentance led to his miraculous renewal.

And today we come to this God. We acknowledge our sin and the fallen condition of this world. We hurt, we are bruised, we have conflict, and we are devastated by God's judgment on our sins. And we say that behind the murder, behind the wars and rumors of wars, behind the abuse, behind the scandal, behind the relationship struggles in our lives, there is sin. If we follow Joel, we will have to declare that behind it all is God himself!

We say that, and our minds cannot fathom it. How can a good God—and before we finish the thought, the truth of Jesus on a cross enters our minds. Before we scandalize God, the cry of God incarnate, nailed to the cross by sinful men, overwhelms all other cries: "'Eli, Eli, lema sabachthani?' that is, 'My God, my God, why have you forsaken me?'" (Matt. 27:46; Mark 15:34).

Behind the Roman nails, behind the plotting of the Jewish religious hierarchy, behind Judas, is God the Father. Who crucified Jesus? The Romans? Yes. The Jewish mobs? Yes. Me? Yes. But behind us all is God. But the sovereignty of God in the cross, judging sin, is the sovereignty of God in salvation, redeeming sinners. It would cause Paul to write: "He who did not spare his own Son but gave him up for us all, how will he not also with him graciously give us all things?" (Rom. 8:32).

In Joel, God is sovereign. And that is our only hope. To bow before this sovereign God is to be risen to new life. To come childlike to this Lord of all is to leave behind the pain of the past, and to be buoyant about the sunlit uplands of life.

Here is the third thing to know about Joel:

3. The locust story is the key to human history, now and forevermore.

That which happened to the ancient people of God, perhaps nine hundred years before the birth of Jesus, is a message for all times.

The people sinned against God by forgetting him and going their own way. God judged the sin and sent the locust. The locusts destroyed the land. The people came together in a worship assembly. There the Lord instructed them to "rend your hearts and not your garments" (2:13a). They were to "return to the LORD, your God, for he is gracious and merciful, slow to anger, and abounding in steadfast love; and he relents over disaster" (2:13b).

The people were saved, and they returned to the land, happy and fulfilled.

Joel used apocalyptic language—mysterious language that nevertheless unveils a future judgment, a future time of returning to God, and a future blessing. Fast-forward nine hundred years or so and you have a remarkable event, a miraculous event happening in Jerusalem. The disciples were gathered after the death, resurrection, and ascension of Jesus. In answer to his promise, the Holy Spirit came down in a new way, a powerful way. When these people began to speak of Jesus, people who spoke other languages could hear them as in their own tongue! When Peter stood up to preach, he said these words of Joel were being fulfilled: "And in those days it shall be, God declares, that I will pour out my Spirit on all flesh, and your sons and your daughters shall prophesy, and your young men shall see visions, and your old men shall dream dreams" (Acts 2:17, quoting Joel 2:28). Peter went on to use the amazing language of Joel:

> I will show wonders in the heavens above
> and signs on the earth below,
> . . . .
> the sun shall be turned to darkness
> and the moon to blood,
> before the day of the Lord comes. (Acts 2:19–20, quoting Joel 2:30–31)

So Peter saw Joel's prophecy fulfilled in Jesus on that very day, the day of Pentecost. The renewing time that followed the locust time in Joel's day was now happening in Peter's day. And we might imagine it will continue until it appears in an even greater way at the second coming of Jesus Christ.

This is what we should remember about Joel:

- The land looms large.
- The Lord stands sovereign.
- The locust story is the key.

Maybe you know people who have been eaten up by locust. Maybe you, like Israel of old, have your heart rent from the pain of sin, or of living in a sinful world. You look up like those saints of old to find God in the midst of your locust-filled lives—with your childhood disappointments, with your affairs and divorce, with your wayward children, and with your unfulfilled dreams. But this is where we hear God calling us to come from those locust fields of our lives. "Call a sacred assembly," and come to him. "Come to me, all who labor and are heavy laden, and I will give you rest" (Matt. 11:28).

Yet as you come, you want to know how God can restore to you the years the locust has eaten. How can God renew your life, pour out his Spirit on you, and make you a new creation?

Two Glorious Ways God Restores the Years the Locusts Have Eaten

1. God's salvation reverses the order of devastation.

In Joel 2:25, God says that he will restore the years the locusts have eaten. He gives a list of the types of locusts, or perhaps their stage of development or their order of attack on the land. In this list, however, there is a reversal of the order introduced in Joel 1:4.

- In Joel 1:4, the prophet describes the onslaught of the insects as "the cutting locust, . . . the swarming locust."
- In Joel 2:25, he describes the judgment now removed as "the swarming locust . . . and the cutter."

God reverses the order. Years of agricultural production were lost. But in God's mercy, he gave future years of great harvest. Animals were lost due to the drought, but water would again flow. There were years of heartache, but the years of joy were on their way.

In his wonderful commentary on Joel, David Prior uses concepts we understand, like "compensation" and "restitution," to describe what God is doing.[11] Many groups want reparation for damage done to them in the past. In this biblical case, God doesn't have to be sued to give reparation. He willingly and graciously gives his restoration, compensation, and reparation out of his steadfast love, his covenant love for his people.

So, too, God will reverse the order of destruction in your life. He will restore your years. You have lost time because of sin, but he will repay you with more time of blessing. In one way or another, he will do it in your life.

I know of a pastor who was discredited by his sin and is now a door-to-door insurance salesman. He has found joy in preaching to street people. I know of a man who went bankrupt, but who now counts himself a wealthy man from preaching the gospel on every continent. I know of a woman who led a life of promiscuity, and who now leads little children in Sunday school. But you may say, "I am about to die, and my life is filled with regret! What can God do for me?" God has eternity to use you, my friend.

God restores to us, in Jesus Christ, the years the locusts have eaten. He reverses the order of things. In short, Jesus redeems us, body and soul, in our lives and in our relationships. A new heaven and a new earth will continue his redeeming work. The way to receive this reversal of sin's effect is to rend your heart before God. Tell him about your hurt and your pain, and confess your sins. Confess your sin of unbelief that he could do anything with your life. Receive his salvation and let the reversal begin.

Now here is the second thing to remember about this passage for your life:

2. God's sovereignty rewrites your story.

God is sovereign in your life, whether you crown him as such or not. His sovereignty does not depend on our ability to discern it or even to believe it. But when we do receive him as Lord of every area of our lives, the power of the truth begins to set us free, just as Jesus promised.

As God was sovereign in the locusts coming to the people in Joel's day, so has he been sovereign in your life, even in the painful places of your past. You may say, "But Israel sinned! I did not sin by being abused!" No, of course not. But we live in a fallen world, where others have sinned. It was not fair that you didn't get the job because of your faith, or that your parents divorced, or that you were crippled from the accident. These things are not your own fault. But until we come to the place where we bow before the sovereign God and say, "Lord, I do not understand why, but I believe you were there," we will not find healing. The sovereignty of God gives us peace. He is the one to right the wrongs, to judge the sinners, and to avenge the wrongdoing. And he will. That is not our business. Our business, if we are to be healed, is to come to God and trust him in our past, and to surrender the unconquerable mysteries of life to him. The cross of Jesus is the place to bring such questions.

> On a hill far away stood an old rugged cross,
> The emblem of suff'ring and shame;
> And I love that old cross where the dearest and best
> For a world of lost sinners was slain.
>
> Oh, that old rugged cross, so despised by the world,
> Has a wondrous attraction for me;
> For the dear Lamb of God left His glory above
> To bear it to dark Calvary.[12]

You can embrace the thing that is hurting you so much and offer it to Jesus Christ as the thing that has brought you to him. You can see the locust's story in your life.

Paul's and Your Testimony of Locust Shells

When Paul writes about the resurrection of Jesus Christ in 1 Corinthians 15, he cannot keep from applying it to his life. You can feel, in Paul's words, the anguish of thinking about the pain of his past and then the release of the power in his new life: "For I am the least of the apostles, unworthy to be called an apostle, because I persecuted the church of God. But by the grace of God I am what I am, and his grace toward me was not in vain" (1 Cor. 15:9–10).

The locusts that ate at Paul were his past sin, his religious zeal without faith, and his persecution of the saints. How devastating were the hordes of locusts that must have eaten at his soul! But through the grace of God in the death, burial, and resurrection of Jesus Christ, God was doing something new in this man's life: "Therefore, if anyone is in Christ, he is a new creation. The old has passed away; behold, the new has come" (2 Cor. 5:17). Do you see what Paul was doing? He was bringing locust shells to God as a gift, a testimony that becomes Paul's praise. This is his locust story.

My Aunt Eva, who reared me, knew about my locust story. She knew about the locusts that came as a result of my sin as a fifteen-year-old prodigal. She knew about my sin and the sins committed against me. And one day, not as a child but as a grown man, I came to her in hurt and pain over the total brokenness in my life. I laid my head on her lap, the pockmarks of the locusts all over me, and I cried. I cried for what seemed like a long time. She told me that God was not finished with me. She told me, in so many words, to go up yonder to that assembly where God's people were gathered. She told me to go to Calvary's cross, to the very person of Jesus Christ and be healed. There, in that place, the little Tabernacle Church, locusts were devoured as saints sang "Just As I Am, Without One Plea." The dark, massive swarms were dispersed and killed by the joyous testimonies of the goodness of God by the poor people in that place. Oh, how I recall the new lives won to Jesus in that poor little tabernacle where I grew up.

It took some time, but through many trials and mistakes, yet through many more mercies, God brought me to see the locust story in my life. Today he has restored to me the years the locusts had eaten. And it is all because of the love of God.

Today I would gladly take a million locust shells to Aunt Eva if she were still sitting in that chair in our backyard. I would tell her just how good the Lord has been to me. But I will not go to her, for she is with God. I will go to Jesus today in prayer with the locust shell of childhood hurt. I will hate the sin, but love the sovereignty that used the sin to bring me to the Lord. The locust has gone out of that shell. I have never been loved and cared for as I have by Jesus Christ. I will go to him with the locust shell of the loneliness of being an orphan. I will bless his name, for I know now I was never really an orphan. I was a child with a heavenly Father. The locust is gone out of that shell. I bless the name of Jesus, for he gave me a wife and children and grandchildren. He gave me spiritual children in my role as a pastor and as a servant at a seminary of young men and women going into ministry. I bless his holy name, for that locust shell is empty. And oh, what glory! The crusty old locust shell has become a horn of plenty, filled with the unmerited blessings of God!

What is the locust in your life? God invites you right here, right now, to let him come into your life and forgive you, accept you, and love you through his Son, Jesus Christ. He wants you to hear his Word:

I will restore to you the years that the . . . locust has eaten,

. . . .

You shall . . . be satisfied,
> and praise the name of the LORD your God,
> who has dealt wondrously with you.
And [you] shall never again be put to shame.
> (Joel 2:25–27)

I will be with you. I will not leave you or forsake you.
> (Josh. 1:5)

Take him your testimony; take him the stories he is writing in your life. Run like a child and give him a basket of locust shells, testimonies of his grace. Heaven, one day, will be like Aunt Eva's apron, filled with locust shells, signs of God's redeeming grace in Jesus Christ in our lives. Will you now hear the horn blowing out the good news in the life, death, and resurrection of Jesus Christ? Will you believe in "a land of beginning again"? "Therefore, if anyone is in Christ, he is a new creation. The old has passed away; behold, the new has come" (2 Cor. 5:17).

Here is a prayer for you to offer to your heavenly Father:

> Lord of the locusts, who has dispersed the dark creatures and their meaning in our lives, all sin and sorrow, through the giving of your only Son, our Savior Jesus Christ, who lived a sinless life, died a sinner's death for me on the cross, rose again from the dead to give me new life, come to me today and
>> renew our land,
>> refresh my life,
>> regenerate my soul,
>> restore my faith,

so that I, with all of your saints, may know and declare that there is a God in Israel who saves to the uttermost. Through Jesus Christ our Redeemer I pray. Amen.

Questions for Reflection

1. If the Hebrew *ha'arets* (the land) is not simply real estate, but the place where our life is lived, describe what it is in your life. Remember: it is not simply geography.
2. Has your "land" ever been attacked or destroyed? How difficult was life to sustain then? Is the picture of restoration in Joel 2:24–27 your experience? If not yet, does it give you hope?
3. The prophet Joel declares that God is sovereign over destruction, as well as over recovery and restoration. Many believers chafe at this hard teaching. What is your reaction and why?
4. When God uses people as instruments of destruction and judgment, does he still hold them accountable for their sin? Is that fair? Explain.
5. David Prior writes, "The steadfast love and compassion of our Father God drives Him in all His dealings with His people." How can this be true in the face of wars, abuse, scandal, and relationship troubles? Have you recognized this truth when you looked back after a time of suffering in your life? Were you able to see it during that time?
6. If the crucifixion of Jesus was the ultimate paradigm for suffering, who was ultimately responsible for it? How does the crucifixion flesh out

the familiar passage in Romans 8:28, "And we know that for those who love God all things work together for good, for those who are called according to his purpose." For whose good was God at work in the crucifixion?

7. Peter saw the day of Pentecost—when the Holy Spirit was poured out—as a fulfillment of Joel's prophecy of renewal and restoration of what the locust had eaten (Acts 2:18–21). Has the Holy Spirit ever "rolled up his sleeves" and restored a locust-eaten area of your life? If so, explain. If not, ask him to come alongside and help you now. Be ready to cooperate.

8. Are there damages in your past for which you want compensation or restitution? Where or to whom have you been looking for reparation? If it hasn't come, where or to whom do you think you can turn for satisfaction?

9. Have you been guilty of the sin of not believing that God can use you because of damage suffered in the past from your own sin or the sin of another? Do you still think this way? If so, are you ready to confess the sin of unbelief? Once you do, watch expectantly for reversal to begin.

10. Is it difficult to bow before a sovereign God and acknowledge that he was present even as you suffered at the hand of someone else? Why is such an acknowledgment—though difficult— essential for lasting peace and healing to enter your life?

11. How is the thing that hurt you so deeply, once offered to Jesus, like a locust shell?

12. What does it mean to hate the sin (yours or that of others), but to love the sovereignty that uses the sin to bring you to the Lord? Give an example from your life or from the life of someone else.

13. Do you have a locust shell to lay at God's feet in praise and worship?

8

A CHRIST FOR CRIPPLED LAMBS AND LAME PRIESTS

Leviticus 21:16–18; 22:21; 2 Corinthians 5:21;
Colossians 1:21–22

There is only one thing I know of that crushes me to the ground and humiliates me to the dust, and that is to look at the Son of God, and especially contemplate the cross. . . . Nothing else can do it. When I see that I am a sinner . . . that nothing but the Son of God on the cross can save me, I'm humbled to the dust. . . . Nothing but the cross can give us this spirit of humility.
—*Dr. Martyn Lloyd-Jones*[1]

Let's Talk About it

As books of the Bible go, Leviticus is not the life of the party. You have to wade through a lot of animal sacrifices, purification rites, and other ceremonial things to get to the divine point of the book. But there is a point, a very important point. Much of the ceremonial statutes, priestly regulations, dietary prohibitions, and penal laws have to do with the holiness of God.

There was a time when I had a real problem with Leviticus, and I want to tell you about how the Lord dealt with me. I think he could deal with you too. As Ben Haden used to say, "Let's talk about it."

> And the LORD spoke to Moses, saying, "Speak to Aaron, saying, None of your offspring throughout their generations who has a blemish may approach to offer the bread of his God. For no one who has a blemish shall draw near, a man blind or lame, or one who has a mutilated face or a limb too long. . . ."
> "And when anyone offers a sacrifice of peace offerings to the LORD to fulfill a vow or as a freewill offering from the herd or from the flock, to be accepted it must be perfect; there shall be no blemish in it." (Lev. 21:16–18; 22:21)

> "For our sake he made him to be sin who knew no sin, so that in him we might become the righteousness of God." (2 Cor. 5:21)

> "And you, who once were alienated and hostile in mind, doing evil deeds, he has now reconciled in his body of flesh by his death, in order to present you holy and blameless and above reproach before him." (Col. 1:21–22)

In this chapter I want to share with you how my story of pain changed to God's story of grace. And then I want us to consider the new life that God promises.

148

"I Had No Idea God Could Use Me!"

There are times when I think to myself, "I have known God's call on my life, to preach the gospel, ever since I can remember." I mean, I think back through my life, and even in my childhood, as I suffered abuse, I knew. Under Aunt Eva's godly guidance, her teaching, times in her lap learning the Scriptures, I knew. And I know this sounds unorthodox, but even when I was a prodigal child, I think I knew. I knew that God had placed his hands on me, like Jeremiah, before I was born, and he had ordained me to proclaim the unsearchable riches of Jesus Christ to others. Of course, according to God's timetable, I had to experience those riches myself. I had to know of the yearning of the soul for God. I had to personally experience the pain and hellishness of being apart from God. I had to know the joy of coming home to the Father and being accepted because of his love and grace alone. I had to be able to love the bride of Christ. I had to be able to say with David, "How lovely is your dwelling place, O Lord of hosts! My soul longs, yes, faints, for the courts of the Lord" (Ps. 84:1–2).

And so, after a life of abuse, heartache, and personal failure, I came to receive God's gracious gift, to trust in Christ alone for eternal life and to become his true disciple. I came to follow him and lead others to him. I sat under the preaching ministry of Robert Baxter (Pastor Bob) in Olathe, Kansas, and grew to love the warm and winsome understanding of the old Reformed faith, with its emphasis upon God's grace.[2] I sought to walk in the "old paths" and relish them.[2] I followed the Lord through the pain of my past. And the pain of my past became the pathway to earnest prayer. My wife and I had committed our lives to Jesus Christ, no matter where that took us.

For the time being, we had followed him in my career as a manager at a Fortune 500 company. My career was soaring in many ways. But I knew. I knew God was calling me. Later I would come to understand how John Calvin would speak of having to have both an inward call and an outer call. The inward call is that "still small voice" that checks your spirit, redirects you to God in prayer, gets your attention, arrests you, and causes you to look upward. The outward call is the consent of God's people to an inner call—the practical, the circumstantial, all working together like planets in orbit, miraculously aligning so as to not miss the effect of providence. One friend of mine describes this outward call as a "parade of providence" marching through our lives. I began to think about surrendering to God's call to preach his gospel. During those days, in the 1980s, I also began to recognize God's outward calling to me. It came through sweet little old ladies in the back of the Sunday school class (God's secret agents, or better yet, angelic hosts!) who would approach me afterward to speak to me.

"Son, have you ever given serious thought to the ministry?"

"Yes, ma'am, I have."

"Well, I think you are the kind of man the church needs. If you were ever to go off to seminary, we would want to help."

Those kinds of encouraging words came frequently to me. My wife, Mae, also knew of this call. She encouraged me in it and believed that this is where the Lord would lead us. She once told me, when I was selling chemicals, that "one day you will have something far greater to talk to others about." My wife, a preacher's daughter, always knew.

It is not like I surrendered immediately. I went through my "Jonah" days. Jonah, of course, when called by God to take the gospel to the great but wicked city of Nineveh, wanted to go in the opposite direction. He bought a one-way ticket to Tarshish. My attempt to run from God caused me to apply to the University of Kansas Law School. When I told my wife, she just looked at me and responded, "Why would you go to law school? You have a career now that is doing well. But this is not about your career, is it? You are running from God." The application to law school was immediately withdrawn, and I sought an appointment with Pastor Bob.

Here is why I was running: I had no idea that God could use me or would use me. The mistakes I had made, the sins I had committed, and the sins committed against me, all seemed to add up to a "no go" for the ministry. During this time, I also read the many opinions about qualifications for the ministry. There seemed to be two great schools of thought. Some felt that a man coming from a life of failure in family and personal life could possibly go into the ministry, given certain conditions, and provided that time had elapsed with a proof of a new life, or "a long obedience in the same direction" (to use Eugene Peterson's wonderful title from his book on Christian discipleship). Then there were others who simply saw certain sins, certain life events even out of one's control, as disqualifying one from gospel ministry.

I had read about Augustine and his sins—sins in regard to women—and yet how God used that broken man to advance his kingdom. I had read about John Newton and his prior life of shame as a profligate sailor—who sinned in ways that are sadly common to ungodly sailors in ports around the world—and yet how God had saved him and then used him mightily as a parish minister in the Church of England. He was the man who would pen the most famous hymn in the Christian world, "Amazing Grace." And of course I knew about Peter and his blasphemy and abandonment of Christ at the cross. I knew of Saul's sin of persecuting Christians and putting them to death, and his participation in the martyrdom of Stephen. I knew of the failed marriage of John Wesley, and how God continued to use that great (and controversial) man.[3] So I knew how God used these men in these ways, but I could not get over a certain passage. It may seem odd to you, but I had to deal with this passage:

> And the LORD spoke to Moses, saying, "Speak to Aaron, saying, None of your offspring throughout their generations who has a blemish may approach to offer the bread of his God. For no one who has a blemish shall draw near, a man blind or lame." (Lev. 21:16–18)

As I read those words about the lame priest, and as I read in chapter 22 about the rejection of a lamb with a blemish, condemning words pounded in my beleaguered brain: "Unholy! Unfit! Crippled! Lame! Unusable!"

I was a lame man, lame from my sin and the sins of others. Of course the priest himself could not help his lameness, and in a sense my life and the pain of my life were beyond me. But here I was. I seemed to be no different from lame men who were denied the old covenant priesthood because of their deformity. My deformity was the deformity of a man who had sinned and who had been sinned against, as well as just dark circumstances arising out of a fallen world that had hurt me. I felt like a crippled lamb. I was the lame priest. Those months when I dealt with this issue were the most tormented time in my life. Indeed, it was this pain, this question resulting from my own ill-informed exegesis that caused a spiritual blockage. That blockage would not allow the free flow of God's grace to feed my soul, and would not allow his call to proceed. This is the real reason I wanted to run. I didn't want to face this pain, this question. I was the crippled lamb that was unacceptable to God. I was the lame priest who was unusable by the Lord.

I thank God for two mercies: First, for Edmund Clowney's beautiful little book, *Called to the Ministry*.[4] That little book by the esteemed late theologian, pastor, and seminary president, helped to clarify and solidify my sense of inner call. I came to see that, with Martin Luther, though I may be gifted to pursue a variety of other vocations, because I have been gifted to preach, I am in the chains of the gospel. "Woe to me if I preach not the gospel of Christ" (from 1 Cor. 9:16). But the chains of Christ are velvet chains. And in these chains I have found my freedom. I put down Dr. Clowney's book and knew that Christ had called me to preach. I felt free to leave all else behind and follow him. But the real issue remained.

And thus the second grace of this period in my life was, once again, found during time spent with Pastor Bob. I came to him with the "lame priest" passage from Leviticus. Pastor Bob told me the difference between Old and New Testament law.[5] He showed me how those old signs and shadows foretold and portrayed the perfect High Priest, Jesus, the Son of God. He also showed me—indeed, he preached the passage to me personally—that when we receive Jesus Christ, his perfect life is given to us. Our sins are laid upon him on the cross. By faith we become, positionally in Christ, a member of Christ's redeemed people and "holy" before the Lord. He stressed that in Christ I was a new creation: "Therefore, if anyone is in Christ, he is a new creation. The old has passed away; behold, the new has come" (2 Cor. 5:17).

I praise God for the truth of Christ's work of redeeming "crippled lambs" and "lame priests":

> Once you were alienated from God and were enemies in your minds because of your evil behavior. But now he has reconciled you by Christ's physical body through death to present you holy in his sight, without blemish and free from accusation. (Col. 1:21–22 NIV)

But there was more than just being positionally holy before God through Christ. God's grace liberated me to preach to others and was the power plant of my ministry. Pastor Bob also told me that instead of ignoring the pain of my past, I must embrace it. My weaknesses, through Christ, would become the very thing that God would use to link my life, as a pattern of God's grace, to the lives of other wounded people. He believed that God was calling me to preach the gospel—indeed, was calling me to the unique ministry of Word and sacrament—and that I must always pastor and preach out of my brokenness. I left his office with a new love for Jesus. I saw my Savior as the one who took my sin and became my righteousness. He was my righteousness for the ministry. He was my new reputation. He was my new credentials. I have no other. I have nothing and I am nothing outside of Jesus Christ.

I want to say with David:

> I will extol the LORD at all times;
>   his praise will always be on my lips.
> My soul will boast in the LORD;
>   let the afflicted hear and rejoice. (Ps. 34:1–2 NIV)

Now I understand the personal passion in Paul when he gave his raison d'être: "I have been crucified with Christ. It is no longer I who live, but Christ who lives in me. And the life I now live in the flesh I live by faith in the Son of God, who loved me and gave himself for me" (Gal. 2:20).

Along with Paul I praise God that Christ has called sinners saved by grace to preach his wonderful good news:

> I thank Christ Jesus our Lord, who has given me strength, that he considered me faithful, appointing me to his service. Even though I was once a

155

blasphemer and a persecutor and a violent man, I was shown mercy because I acted in ignorance and unbelief. The grace of our Lord was poured out on me abundantly, along with the faith and love that are in Christ Jesus.

Here is a trustworthy saying that deserves full acceptance: Christ Jesus came into the world to save sinners—of whom I am the worst. But for that very reason I was shown mercy so that in me, the worst of sinners, Christ Jesus might display his unlimited patience as an example for those who would believe on him and receive eternal life. (1 Tim. 1:12–16 NIV)

Now, it is not given to all to preach the gospel as an ordained minister, but we all have a call to be his witnesses and to show forth his grace and mercy to others. And the very thing that has hurt you the most, where you feel most vulnerable, is the area where Christ has shown you so much grace. This is your God-given connecting point to other human beings. Our essential humanity transcends all cultures and all races and all generations and times. And the gospel is clear on these points:

We have a problem.
According to the Bible, that problem is our sin. As Paul writes, "For all have sinned and fall short of the glory of God" (Rom. 3:23).

We know that our past condemns us, our future is thus uncertain, and today is not looking so good. Our past is bogging down our present and clogging up our future. We know this. We feel this. This is why God gave us Leviticus. Here we are shown the holiness of God and the sinfulness of man. Here we are shown, through the pictorial representation of perfect lambs and perfect priests that God cannot be approached but in perfect holiness.

Therefore we also learn:

We need a High Priest.

We long for someone who can take care of these things for us. In our more self-deluded moments, we imagine that we can take care of these things ourselves. We suppose that with a little religion, and with a reputation we carefully construct, we can make ourselves presentable to God.

There is a Civil War–era house in Franklin, Tennessee. One of the most remarkable features of this house is the bloodstains on the wooden floor from when the house was a field hospital during the Battle of Franklin. It is amazing to me that through all the years since then, and with all the residents and visitors, those stains are still there.

That is the way our sin is. A little religion can't get rid of the stains of sin, and a good reputation cannot erase secret sin. You can hire the greatest image consultant in the world, and he can fix some external things for you, but he cannot deal with your heart.

We need a sacrifice.

The passages in Leviticus teach us the importance of a payment. All of the prohibitions, regulations, and ceremonies are there because of the holiness of God and the sinfulness of man. Only a holy lamb could ceremonially take the place of, and atone for, the sins of unholy people. There had to be a holy priesthood,

157

even pure in body, to paint God's picture of the kind of man who was needed to offer atonement for our sins.

God gave us what we need in Jesus.

Jesus is our perfect priest, who is the Mediator between God and man. This is what the writer to the Hebrews declares: "For it was indeed fitting that we should have such a high priest, holy, innocent, unstained, separated from sinners, and exalted above the heavens" (Heb. 7:26). He is at once God and man, with his face to God pleading his own blood for our sins, and with his face to man, giving us the word of forgiveness, which sets us free.

And again Paul summed it up with these words: "For our sake he [God] made him [Jesus] to be sin who knew no sin, so that in him we might become the righteousness of God" (2 Cor. 5:21). What God has demanded, he has provided through his only begotten Son, that whosoever believes in him should not perish but have eternal life.

J. Gresham Machen was one of the most amazing men of the twentieth century, though relatively few know of him today.[6] An outstanding New Testament scholar at Princeton, and a stalwart in promoting the work of foreign missions, Machen was also the key intellectual figure in the modernist-fundamentalist debates. He went so far as to write a book called *Christianity and Liberalism*. If you think about his title, you will understand where he was coming from. He insisted that ministers had to affirm the "fundamentals" of the faith, such as the virgin birth, the resurrection, and the divinity of Jesus, or they were not truly Christian ministers. He actively opposed the way the Presbyterian Church in the U.S.A. was sending out foreign missionaries who did not believe these fundamental doctrines, and so he was defrocked and forced out of Princeton. He founded Westminster Seminary. And this is where I am going with this story: on a winter trip in the Dakotas, to preach and raise interest in the seminary, he fell seriously ill. He knew he was near death. So he sent what would be his final text. Before he died on January 1, 1937, Dr. Machen sent a telegram to a fellow professor at Westminster, and his final words were, "I'm so thankful for the active obedience of Christ. No hope without it."[7]

Some might find this a rather cryptic statement. What did he mean by the active obedience of Jesus Christ? Machen was speaking of what Bible scholars refer to as Christ's active and passive obedience. His active obedience is needed for our salvation, for we are to be holy just as God is holy. Thus we read: "For as by the one man's disobedience the many were made sinners, so by the one man's obedience the many will be made righteous" (Rom. 5:19).

The passive obedience of Jesus was his dying on the cross for our sins. And so we read: "And being found in appearance as a man, he humbled himself and became obedient to death—even death on a cross!" (Phil. 2:8 NIV).

Jesus fulfilled two great needs for us: He lived the life we could not live (his active obedience). He also died on the cross to atone for our sins (his passive obedience).

Machen, as he looked forward to the day when he would stand before almighty God, stated simply that the holiness of Jesus was his only hope.

This is what we are talking about. Jesus is our unblemished Lamb, the righteousness we need. When by faith we receive this Lamb, he takes away our sins, and his pure white life is placed over ours, so that God sees Christ in us when we have received him.

That is the sum of all of this. Today, through faith in Jesus, through his obedience and death on the cross, you are free:

- You are free to serve Christ regardless of what your past sins are, for he took them, and you live now as a person under his righteousness, not your own.
- You are free to follow the law of God; because he has saved you by grace, you may now, out of thanksgiving, out of overflowing love, seek to follow the teaching of Jesus Christ.
- You are free to let go of oppressive legalistic thinking that has held you in bondage to thinking you have to earn your place as a son or daughter.
- You are free to embrace the power of the gospel that alone can snap the chains of unholy powers, like physical, emotional, and even behavioral addictions.
- You are free from fear of death or hell or even the condemnation of others.

In a word, you are free to live.

Did you ever see that old commercial for Nestea, where the hot sun is bearing down on a sun-baked fellow who just collapses backwards in the cool refreshment of a swimming pool? The gospel of Jesus Christ allows you today to collapse into the unfathomable grace of God and be washed clean and made new. I love the way the young Scottish minister Robert Murray M'Cheyne put it: "Unfathomable oceans of grace are in Christ for you."[8]

And from this pool of grace, poured out from the life of our Lord Jesus Christ, we are made whole—all of us crippled lambs and lame priests.

Questions for Reflection

1. Do you think it is necessary to actually experience the pain of being apart from God and the joy of returning to him before being used by God to lead others to him? Why or why not? If not necessary, could the experience provide any advantage?
2. How does the pain of the past become the pathway to earnest prayer? What are some "places" to which such a pathway to prayer might lead?
3. Can you identify with the outward call of God as "a parade of providence marching through your life"? If so, describe your experience. If not, pray for the Holy Spirit to make you attentive to the strains of the march in the distance.
4. Eugene Peterson wrote about "a long obedience in the same direction." Does that mean a Christian never falters or reverses direction? Explain.
5. How did John Newton's former life as an ungodly sailor aid him in writing the hymn *Amazing Grace*? Is there something in your past or present situation that might be offered to God for transformation into something that he could use to bless others?

6. Are there any condemning words pounding in your brain and causing a "spiritual blockage"? If so, begin today to replace those old tapes— one statement at a time—with truths about how God sees you and precious promises he has made to you. Begin with 2 Corinthians 5:17, "Therefore, if anyone is in Christ, he is a new creation. The old has passed away; behold, the new has come."

7. What does the following statement mean? "The chains of Christ are velvet chains." When we become captive to Christ, are we more or less free than before?

8. Has God ever used a weakness of yours to link your life, as a pattern of his grace, to the life of someone else? Can you elaborate? If he hasn't done so yet, ask the Holy Spirit to show you if there is something standing in the way.

9. Once we receive Christ as our Savior, he becomes our righteousness, reputation, and credentials. Does this mean it is not necessary to read and study the Bible? Why or why not?

10. "The very thing that has hurt you the most, where you feel most vulnerable, is the area where Christ has shown you so much grace. This is your God-given connecting point to other human beings." Can you identify one or more of your own connecting points? If it is easier to see them in the lives of others than in your own, ask a trusted spiritual friend what he or she sees as yours.

11. Is it fair of God to require perfection (see Lev. 21 and 22)? Why or why not? And if that is the mark, where is hope to be found?

12. What is meant by the active obedience of Christ, and why is that important to you? How does it relate to his passive obedience? Why are both essential if we are to have hope as we stand before God?

13. If Christ's active and passive obedience combine to free you from an eternity in hell, what do they free you to do right now?

PART 5

PAIN AND PRAISE IN BROKEN RELATIONSHIPS

9

WHAT GOD STARTS, GOD COMPLETES: MY TESTIMONY TO THE SAVING WORK AND KEEPING POWER OF JESUS CHRIST

Philippians 1:6

Being confident of this very thing, that He who has begun a good work in you will complete it until the day of Jesus Christ.
—*Philippians 1:6 NKJV*

The Heart of My Ministry

Imagine reading the psalms of David without knowing the presence and power of God in David's own life. Imagine reading the epistles of Paul without knowing the history of God's grace and mercy in Paul's life. Imagine reading Peter's bold declaration about "a living hope through the resurrection of Jesus Christ from the dead" (1 Peter 1:3) and yet being ignorant of the grace he received after his glaring sin of denying that he knew Jesus.

The power of the message of these men is communicated to us in an even greater way because we realize that they knew grace personally. They had encountered the life-changing power of Jesus Christ in their own lives. Their personal testimony really formed the very heart of their ministries.

I would prefer that people read my curriculum vitae with an awareness of the presence and power of Jesus Christ in my life. My ministry is more than degrees, credentials, and personal statistics. It is the story of my encounter with the resurrected Jesus Christ. It only makes sense when one knows the reality of Christ alive in me.

Here, then, is my testimony. This is the heart of my ministry.

And let me introduce the heart of my ministry with the heart of God that beats in me out of his Word. The most memorable Scripture verses are those that seem to speak timeless truth to every generation in just a few words.

The Lord is my shepherd; I shall not want. (Ps. 23:1)

For God so loved the world, that he gave his only Son, that whoever believes in him should not perish but have eternal life. (John 3:16)

And we know that all things work together for good to those who love God, to those who are the called according to His purpose. (Rom. 8:28 NKJV)

And the verse before us:

> Being confident of this very thing, that He who has begun a good work in you will complete it until the day of Jesus Christ. (Phil. 1:6 NKJV)

In a church where I pastored, I saw a little boy coming out of Sunday school carrying a craft project that I will never forget. It was a piece of colored paper with road construction signs all over it and his picture in the middle. At the bottom in glitter it read, "Please be patient. God is not finished with me yet."

The passage before us is one of my favorite passages. In it Paul, that great encourager of the saints, begins his "letter of joy" in the epistle to the church at Philippi by seeking to stir up confidence in people who were feeling a little shaken about some problems in their church. They had given him a financial gift, and he in return gave them a gift: life-changing spiritual food. In essence, he told them, "Please be patient with yourself. God is not finished with you yet." I want to use this passage to encourage you in facing your problems.

A lady once came to me for counseling. She had just become a Christian, and felt that her life had been lived so far from God that she could never "catch up." In fact, she told me, through many tears, "I will never have a Christian home. I can never hope to live a happy Christian life. I'm just too messed up."

I told her that God had started a great work in her, and that he would never let her go. "In fact," I said, "he is at work, even now, completing what he started. He is making something beautiful of your life."

She asked me, "How can you be sure?"

I told her this story.

The Power of God at Work in One Life

He was born to an aging alcoholic career naval officer and an uneducated half-breed Choctaw Indian from Mississippi. They had met in an alcoholics' recovery program, and with nothing else in common but their pain, they conceived a child. Despite attempts by the mother to abort the child, the father's insistence won out. Amid rumor, scandal, confusion, and embarrassment, a little boy was born in New Orleans, Louisiana, in the late 1950s.

It was soon apparent that this union, begun in pain, would end in pain. The child only complicated an otherwise hopeless situation.

At first the mother kept the child, but after her alcoholism bred schizophrenia, she abandoned him while the father was out to sea. According to one family account, she once hid her son in a doghouse. Mercifully, the police located him. Needing to return to the sea to earn a living, the father turned to his sister back home in rural eastern Louisiana. Having just lost her husband and with no children of her own, that sixty-five-year-old woman took the little fellow in. There on a little chicken farm in the tall piney woods of the Louisiana-Mississippi border country, the widow and the little boy began their new life together.

The first few years were difficult for the lad. His mother took him away several times, usually beating him with the buckle end of a belt until he bled. For years the child would have nightmares of those beatings. Finally, the courts made him a ward of his aunt, and he would not know his biological mother again until years later.

When he was only six, the boy saw his father, who had been discharged from active duty because of medical problems related to his alcoholism, accept an invitation from the aunt to go to church, just up the gravel road from where they lived. The three of them—the alcoholic father, his widowed sister, and the little boy—walked toward the country church. That Wednesday night, when the lay preacher, a plumber by day, began to open up the Scriptures in his sermon, the little boy watched his father kneel in the sawdust of that rough-hewn "tabernacle."

He witnessed his daddy weeping in repentance and faith and saw the lay preacher come down from the pulpit and lay his hands on the head of the weeping man. The boy's daddy confessed his sins and pleaded, through heaving tears, to Jesus Christ to forgive him and save his soul. Within a few months, his father, sober and living for Christ, fell victim to the years of alcohol abuse. That little boy would never forget the cold spring rain falling upon the steel gray casket of his new Christian father as it was lowered into the ground at the Methodist churchyard in Walker, Louisiana.

One year later, the boy made a public profession of faith in Christ. His aunt would never miss one day of reading the Bible to him and laying her hands on him to pray. Jesus Christ was as close as a brother. Yet for all of her love and all the benefits of being in a Christian home, a recurring thought, a thought that he could not shake, haunted the little boy: *I am a child with no parents; I am a loser.*

In spite of that, it was a real Huck Finn existence for the lad in that backwoods country. It was the poorest parish in the state of Louisiana, but life felt very rich—

rivers to cross, fish to catch, cows to chase, and old dogs to love. Books fed the boy's imagination about faraway places, and he dreamed of becoming a superhero.

By the age of six he had won a poetry competition put on by the local electric co-op. At seven he had won a prize in an art competition. He was also beginning to show signs of promise in athletics.

By age twelve he was a baseball all-star, MVP for the Little League, and MVP for Pee Wee football. Soon he would go to the state high school baseball championships as the youngest high school starter in the state of Louisiana. As a fullback, he became the leading rusher in the district, and major universities were scouting him as early as the ninth grade.

He was also active in 4-H club. His calf won every contest, and he and the Hereford, Little Joe, traveled far and wide, taking home a sack full of blue ribbons.

However, there was a problem. He was becoming distant from the childhood relationship with the God of his aunt. Though still very active in church life, he began to remove himself from church friends, choosing rather to associate with those who challenged authority.

Soon his interests in football, 4-H, and drawing were replaced by an interest in music. He preferred the deep and dark folk strains of the late 1960s. He began to delve into a world of darkness: new philosophies, drinking, smoking, and roaming around at late hours of the night. He was somehow kept from drugs and jail, but new interests in abstract art and underground music, which so reflected his own confusion, soon possessed him like a demon from hell and sucked promise and potential and sound judgment from his young life.

This increasingly confused and wayward young man, within only weeks of his seventeenth birthday and against the wishes of his dear old aunt and the little country church, left home in unbelief. His aunt cried out a warning that his action, which included a relationship that she could not approve of, would bring him the greatest pain in his life and would break him. She told him that one day he would have to come home, and when he did, it would be in brokenness. He thought he knew better, and he left.

The young man would later say that this period of his life was eerily similar to his own parents' confused lives. Both were in rebellion, and pain was their marked commonality. Tragedy, struggle, and conflict marked all of his relationships. At one time or another the young man was guilty of or endured drunkenness, pornography, adultery, abandonment, and even violence. There was good that came in the birth of three children during this period of his life. All profoundly deaf, they became the center of the young man's world. But that, too, would one day be lost.

In a little Episcopal church in Morgan City, Louisiana, the young man, then in his early twenties, heard the words of Jesus Christ during a morning prayer service. For him, it was the moment of awakening. Like the prodigal son in the far country who recognized his desperate plight, this young man saw his sinful life flash before him. He began a deliberate journey back to the father's home, which would take several more years. At that point he was awakened to his sin, but still searching for home.

The awakening to his sin and his desire to find the God of his childhood and the God of his aunt only complicated matters in his home. Enmity, strife, and adultery were the continued response of that confused young woman to the young searcher's interest in the things of God. At one time, the woman opened the car door as they drove along the highway at seventy miles an hour, threatening to commit suicide unless he renounced Jesus Christ. The problem finally resulted in an attempt to murder the young man. Separation, reconciliation, and more eruptions finally worked together for finality. She moved in with another man. His heart had been ripped out of his chest, and he sank into deep depression. Repeated attempts by his former wife and her new husband to gain full custody of the children finally broke down whatever dignity was left in the young man, and his decision at length sealed the devastating end to an illicit union. He was left with nothing but his life, and recurring thoughts of ending it that were all too real.

There came a time in his life when his aunt's wise words found their meaning and he came home— broken and weeping and tired. She kept telling him, "Son, God's got a plan and it's going to be all right. Remember, he is not finished with you yet."

Slowly but surely the plan began to unfold. He met and, this time with the blessing of his aunt, married a single mother of four and began to settle down. But the pain of the past haunted him. In fact, his entire life kept coming before him with all of its darkness and sorrow.

The new family joined a small church in a rural area outside of Baton Rouge, and the pastor asked the young man, now in his late twenties, to go to an Evangelism Explosion clinic. There he heard the gospel of Jesus Christ presented. For the first time, he actually understood what grace meant—that God in Christ had lived the life he could never live and had given himself as an offering for his own sins.

He understood that it was only through faith and not because of works that anyone was saved. He understood the reality of God's sovereign power. He rushed home to tell his wife, and in joy and awe and wonder they began together to study the doctrines of grace. The sovereignty of God, once a mysterious doctrine, became like medicine to his soul as he realized that the words of his aunt were, in fact, very scriptural when she had said that God had a plan. The Bible said that all things work together for good to those who love God, and that he who started the good work would complete it.

Within only a few days, this sinner saved by grace would begin to share the gospel of Jesus Christ with others. Within two years, he was elected to be an elder at his church, and then, realizing that God had summoned him to a ministry of Word and sacrament, he surrendered to the call to preach. The man left a long career in management, and the family pulled up stakes and went to seminary, where he finished with honors and won the award in theology and preaching. Following seminary, he was accepted into a Ph.D. program at the University of Wales to study theology. Simultaneously, he accepted a call to be a church planter and later became senior minister of that church. By the time he finished his Ph.D. and accepted a call to a seminary to train others, he had led the church into their first building and founded a radio ministry and a new Christian school for the area.

The young woman looked at me, waiting for me to tell her what she had now figured out for herself. I told her, "I am that man."

And What of the People in My Life?

In an interesting twist that only God could write into reality, the mother who had sought to abort me, and who had tied me up and beat me when I was a child, would later be converted to Christ on her deathbed through the witness of the one she once sought to abort. When she died shortly afterward, I preached at her funeral.

In a wonderful act of mercy and grace, God blessed Mae and me with the birth of our son in 1994—John Michael Ellis Milton—named after my father and me. Placed in our arms as an act of grace, John Michael became a sign of God's remarkable gift of love. As Mae would write in her letter to our first church, "I feel like God has kissed our family." It is always amazing to me that God so blessed us that others would seek us out to learn how to rear children and how to have a happy home. But he does, and that, too, is a testimony to God's goodness and his amazing grace.

And what of my aunt? Well, Aunt Eva lived to the age of ninety-eight near her son, the preacher. She was a charter member of the church I planted, and before she passed quietly into glory, she gave us the only earthly possession she could afford to give: her blessing and her charge. "I love you all. Keep up the good work." She fell asleep in Jesus, singing songs of praise. She could see that the plan of God was at work in the life of that boy she had raised for Christ.

What happened to those precious children who were taken from me? At the exact time of my aunt's death, God began to open the door to what had long since closed. On the very day that I conducted my aunt's funeral, a man I had not seen for thirty years approached me. He told me, "I know where the children are." God's mighty hand of providence moved after that—without me lifting one finger—and my wife took a photograph of my reunion with the oldest child in front of her dormitory in Washington, D.C. Later, a letter came from the next one—just starting college and eager to see me. The story is not yet finished, but suffice it to say that after years of prayer and hope in the God of our lives, he is writing another testimony to his grace and mercy and sovereign power. Jessica, Heather, and Matthew are each seeking the Lord, as I did, and finding him faithful as they do.

I say with that little Sunday school boy, "Please be patient. God is not finished with me yet."

I tell you this story, not out of a morbid need to air my messy past, or because I desire to draw your attention to my failures or my accomplishments, but only for this reason: "He who has begun a good work in you will complete it until the day of Jesus Christ" (Phil. 1:6 NKJV). God began the work in my life when I trusted in him so many years ago. His Spirit would not stop seeking me out, and he was there when I left the "far country" to come home to the God of my childhood. He took all of my pain and my mistakes and my sorrow and has—like the wonderful gospel song—made something beautiful of my life.

And what of that woman who came to me with her concern that she could never have a Christian family? I conducted a wedding for her and her Christian groom a year later. On the last day of my pastorate before accepting a call to Knox Seminary, I baptized their little boy. As she looked up at me, I once again saw tears. But this time it was Philippians 1:6 tears. God was completing what he had started in her life.

Let me give you three truths from God's word in Philippians 1:6 that will change your life:

1. First, this passage teaches that God must begin the work—not you.

It is not until you learn and yield to the old Reformed doctrine of God's grace alone that you can enjoy eternal life and assurance of it. Are you perhaps trusting in your works? For years I trusted in the faith of my aunt without understanding it myself, and it cost me dearly. Can you never look back to a time when you recognized that Christ did it all and that you are absolutely dependent upon him alone for works of righteousness and forgiveness of sins?

If so, then do away with your own religion now and turn to the faith taught in God's Word. Do it now. Turn to Jesus Christ and cry out to him alone. Throw your works as far from you as you can. They will bring you nothing but sorrow in this life and eternal sorrow in the life to come. But to know Christ and to trust in him alone is to know the joy of all joys. The invitation is before you.

2. Second, it is comforting to note that God begins the work of salvation "in you"—that is, God works through ordinary sinful and broken folks who turn to him in repentance and faith.

Whatever it is that you have done, he can forgive you and use you in some way. God's grace and mercy are greater than your worst sins. He may not use you as a pastor or teacher, but he will always use you as a witness to his grace. God begins his greatest work in those most greatly crushed. His power is demonstrated in your weakness. I ask you to offer your pain and your heartaches to the only one who can make sense of it. God works through people like you.

3. Third, this passage teaches that God will complete it. God will see you through your every trial.

What a great consolation this is to the life of one who is going through what one ancient writer called "the dark night of the soul." What an encouraging doctrine it is for all who have fallen so deeply into sin that they would have otherwise lost all hope of new life.

This text in Philippians—one of so many—points to the single greatest liberating truth in all of Scripture: the sovereignty of God.

What Does All This Mean? How Does Philippians 1:6 Work in Your Life?

There was once a lumberjack who took his little son with him into the woods for the day. While there, a great storm came up, and the creeks in the woods began to flood. The two were practically trapped between the woods and their home by a swift-moving creek that was rising by the minute. On the bank of that creek the dad took his little son into his arms and held him tightly. The little boy, out of sheer exhaustion, fell asleep on his father's shoulder.

The next thing the boy knew, he was awakened to see the morning sun flooding through the curtains in his room. He was in his own bed, clean, dry, and safe. His father was leaning on the doorway with a mug of coffee in his hand. He was giving the boy his usual first smile of the day.

You see, God's sovereignty is like that. When, in the storms of life, it seems that the problems of life begin to rise so fast that we could never get home again, we can rest in the arms of our all-powerful Father. God will carry us through the worst of storms all the way home.

God began the work in my life, and in the midst of the storms, I finally learned to trust in his sovereign power.

You can do that, too, right now. And you will one day wake up to see that he brought you safely all the way home. His promises bring abundant life here and now, and eternal life with God when we die. I invite those who want to commit their life to Jesus Christ alone for eternal life and those who want to recommit to trusting in the sovereignty of God to join me as I pray:

> Lord of life, we thank you that you have the sovereign power to pick up broken lives and turn them into trophies of grace. We here offer you our lives. We confess that Christ lived the life we can never live and that his death paid the penalty for our sins and that his rising again from the dead secured

our eternal life. Forgive us for unbelief and work
a work of grace in our lives.

Lord of life, use us to tell others and to encourage
others who need healing.

In the name of Jesus Christ our Lord, we pray. Amen.

Questions for Reflection

1. Is it necessary to have a personal knowledge of the
grace of God—to have experienced it—in order
to tell others about it? Why or why not?
2. Have you ever felt, or do you now feel, "too messed
up" to live a happy Christian life? How can being
troubled by such feelings actually serve as an
assurance that God is already working to make
something beautiful of your life?
3. In my testimony to the power of God at work in
my life, where did you first see grace enter? What
or who was the instrument of God's grace? Did
the one whom God used to extend grace to me
receive grace in return? Do you know what it is
like to be on either end of that process?
4. Dark philosophies, abstract art, and underground
music can reflect a life in confusion. Conversely,
the apostle Paul taught, "Do not conform any longer to the pattern of this world, but be transformed
by the renewing of your mind" (Rom. 12:2 NIV).
Since being transformed is a continual process,
what are some habits you can develop to renew
your mind?
5. Some interests and friends have the potential
to suck promise, potential, and sound judgment
from a life. Do you agree? Are there interests and
friends that are having a detrimental effect on

your life or the life of someone you love? What is one step you can take toward healthy change?

6. Have you heard it said that we are what we eat? If tragedy, struggle, and conflict can be food for a relationship, what might grow on such a diet? What are some regular additions to your own "relationship diet" that would constitute healthier fare?

7. Change can begin in a moment of awakening and a sudden recognition of plight, but the desperate journey back to God can take years. Do you see yourself somewhere on that continuum? If not, what would be the first step in a deliberate journey toward God?

8. When we begin acting upon our desire to find God, do our situations and relationships always improve immediately? Why or why not?

9. In the chapter you just read, Aunt Eva was certain that God had a plan and that it would be all right. Was the young man convinced? Are you convinced of that truth for your life? If not, what would convince you?

10. Is the doctrine of the sovereignty of God—knowing that everything that touches your life must first pass through God's hands—medicine for your soul or a tough pill to swallow? Explain.

11. Romans 8:28 assures us that in all things God works for the good of those who love him, and Philippians 1:6 promises that he who began a good work in you will carry it on to completion. Does that mean that only good things come from God? Does it mean that all things that come from God are good? Explain the difference.

12. Can you look back to a time in your life when you recognized your absolute dependency upon Christ for righteousness and forgiveness of your sins? If so, praise God for his grace toward you. If not, upon what have you been depending? Now is the time to turn away from that to Christ alone.

13. "God begins his greatest work in those most greatly crushed." Do you agree? Why or why not? Does having read of my checkered past encourage you to believe that God can use you too?

14. Do you think God is more honored when we thank him for bringing us through a storm or when we trust him in the midst of the storm? Explain.

15. Must all be set right in your life for you to become a trophy of God's grace? Why or why not?

WOUNDED IN THE HOUSE OF FRIENDS: WHAT TO DO WHEN CHRISTIANS HURT YOU

Genesis 50:15–21; Philippians 3:8–10

All the years you have waited for them to "make it up to you" and all the energy you expended trying to make them change (or make them pay) kept the old wounds from healing and gave pain from the past free rein to shape and even damage your life. And still they may not have changed. Nothing you have done has made them change. Indeed, they may never change. Inner peace is found by changing yourself, not the people who hurt you. And you change yourself for yourself, for the joy, serenity, peace of mind, understanding, compassion, laughter, and bright future that you get.
—Lewis B. Smedes[1]

And if one asks him, "What are these wounds on your back?" he will say, "The wounds I received in the house of my friends."
—Zechariah 13:6

Walking Wounded

One second. One mistake. One firing of the missile in the midst of the war. The missile cannot come back. The weapon is now headed for you. And the one who fired it is on your side. It is war. You are hit by friendly fire.

This is not Baghdad or the Battle of the Bulge or Pork Chop Hill. I am speaking of the many walking wounded in the body of Christ who have been hurt by other believers, people who have been hit by the betrayal of a Christian.

But this is no mistake. She meant to say those words. He meant to plot against you. They meant to bring you down. And you will never be the same. You will suffer with this for the rest of your life. You will not go back to any church. You will lick your wounds. Pain will possess you for the rest of your life. And over time the pain turns to bitterness.

Do you know anyone like that? Or is that your story? Are you the victim of a wound inflicted by someone you love?

It does not have to be that way. Let's look at some verses:

> When Joseph's brothers saw that their father was dead, they said, "It may be that Joseph will hate us and pay us back for all the evil that we did to him." So they sent a message to Joseph, saying, "Your father gave this command before he died, 'Say to Joseph, Please forgive the transgression of your brothers and their sin, because they did evil to you.' And now, please forgive the transgression of the servants of the God of your father." Joseph wept when they spoke to

him. His brothers also came and fell down before him and said, "Behold, we are your servants." But Joseph said to them, "Do not fear, for am I in the place of God? As for you, you meant evil against me, but God meant it for good, to bring it about that many people should be kept alive, as they are today. So do not fear; I will provide for you and your little ones." Thus he comforted them and spoke kindly to them. (Gen. 50:15–21)

Some indeed preach Christ from envy and rivalry, but others from good will. The latter do it out of love, knowing that I am put here for the defense of the gospel. The former proclaim Christ out of rivalry, not sincerely but thinking to afflict me in my imprisonment. What then? Only that in every way, whether in pretense or in truth, Christ is proclaimed, and in that I rejoice. Yes, and I will rejoice. (Phil. 1:15–18)

Indeed, I count everything as loss because of the surpassing worth of knowing Christ Jesus my Lord. For his sake I have suffered the loss of all things and count them as rubbish, in order that I may gain Christ and be found in him, not having a righteousness of my own that comes from the law, but that which comes through faith in Christ, the righteousness from God that depends on faith—that I may know him and the power of his resurrection, and may share his sufferings, becoming like him in his death. (Phil. 3:8–10)

Interrupted by God

When I was a pastor, preparing sermons, I generally followed a plan and thought I knew what to preach each week. But then God interrupted my life. And that is the way it should be. I had to drop my plan one week and address a different matter—one that is a universal need in the lives of Christians and, I must say, in the lives of non-Christians.

It is the matter of being hurt by one you love. It is the matter of seeing yourself as a victim—or not—in that process. Let me tell you how God brought this to me, and then I want to address it from God's Word.

One day, among other appointments, I was to meet with three different families. None of them were from our church, or even from our city. Without going into detail, let me also say they were all in full-time ministry.

The first couple began to tell me their story. But soon the words, going nowhere as far as I could tell, ended in tears. They said, "We have been hurt by other Christians." I spent no small amount of time with them. I brought them to God's Word, and we spent time together seeking the truths of Scripture. Our time was over.

Then came the second family. They began a rambling story that got more complicated as they went. I slowed them down and tried to help them identify the heartache. Another believer had betrayed them. I was amazed. Two appointments, two identical issues. But my amazement was not yet complete.

The third person came in. I was almost ready to say, "All right, so how were you hurt by another believer?" But he told me his concern was about a vocational decision. I thought, OK, great, this is not a trend. We spoke about his vocational crisis—seeking God's will on what to do with his life. Finally, holding back tears, he interrupted our flow of talk with the real hurt: "I am in this fix because another Christian hurt me!"

Have you ever been hurt by someone you love? Or respect? Have you ever been disillusioned about the church because you were let down by a leader in the church? Maybe you are a pastor who is not in a pulpit because you have been hurt. I know for a fact that whenever I am addressing missionaries or pastors, and especially pastors' wives and children, these kinds of wounds are present.

I call this "friendly fire." It is the flack that we take from our own side. It is the misguided bomb intended for the enemy that lands right smack-dab in the middle of our hearts. David knew the pain. "Even my close friend in whom I trusted, who ate my bread, has lifted his heel against me" (Ps. 41:9). Our Lord knew the pain. "He who ate my bread has lifted his heel against me" (John 13:18).

Today the question is not "How do we stop it?" The question is "What do we do with it?" The question may also be put, "Will I remain a victim, or will I move to being a victor with Christ?"

When the Clock Stops

I once sold insurance door-to-door in poor areas of Louisiana. One of my clients was a family who lived in an old house on the other side of the tracks. Every month I would go to collect the insurance money, and we would sit in their living room and talk. One day I noticed that the clock was wrong. It said nine o'clock when, in fact, it was noon. I said nothing. But I saw the same thing the next month and then the next month. Finally, I said something to the husband and wife. Tears came to their eyes. "That was the moment our boy died ten years ago," they told me. The clock had stopped in their lives.

The pain of friendly fire is like that. It can stop the clock in your heart. This happens to Christians whom other Christians hurt and who fail to identify their pain with Christ. The clock stops. They go through life, month after month, year after year, and often church after church, but the clock stopped in their lives way back when they were hurt. These days it is popular to be a victim. But being a victim is not a good way to live because life cannot go forward when the clock has stopped at the point of your last betrayal.

Yet I wonder, are you living your life with the clock stopped?

There is another answer. There is a way to healing. But I warn you, it will involve another kind of pain—the pain of Christ's cross. Christ's cross will bring resurrection, and the new life he brings will also make the clock start ticking again.

This is what we see in Joseph's ability to forgive his brothers after they literally ditched him. Joseph identified his pain with God. In God the pain was intended to bring blessing. Being hurt by his brothers made sense. The pain of false accusation made sense. The trial of unjust imprisonment was good. The years of separation from his father were good for him. He was saying with David, "Make us glad for as many days as you have afflicted us, and for as many years as we have seen evil" (Ps. 90:15).

The power at work in the life of Joseph is what you need in order to get past this hurt. It is the power that was present in Paul when he said, "I have been crucified with Christ. It is no longer I who live, but

Christ who lives in me. And the life I now live in the flesh I live by faith in the Son of God, who loved me and gave himself for me" (Gal. 2:20). It is what Paul is getting at in our text from Philippians. By embracing the pain that comes at him as a means of identifying with Jesus Christ, Paul moves from victim to victor.

Let's apply God's Word to this situation. This is for any believer hurt by another believer, for anyone hurt by a loved one, for anyone feeling like a victim of another person or maybe just feeling betrayed by life. In order for you to move from victim to victor in dealing with the pain of betrayal or suffering of any kind, three drastic steps must be taken. We see these three drastic steps being taken by Paul, who was in prison as a result of the plotting of his own people (Phil. 3:10–11), and by Joseph, who was mistreated by his own brothers (Gen. 50:19–20).

First, think about what God teaches victims about this from Philippians 3:

> . . . that I may know him and the power of his resurrection, and may share his sufferings, becoming like him in his death, that by any means possible I may attain the resurrection from the dead. (Phil 3:10–11)

This is your first step when hurt by another.

1. Take up your cross.

Paul is given a cross. His cross is imprisonment. He is imprisoned because of the betrayal and treachery of people who should have loved him and encouraged him. In Philippians 1, it is the betrayal and treachery of fellow preachers of the gospel. In Philippians 3, it is the betrayal and treachery and plotting of the Jews. In so many ways we see this man betrayed, and he is now in prison. Every sorrow, every act of treachery, every act of betrayal has become, for him, a point of identification with Christ. Through these things he knows resurrection in his life.

But Paul will say, "I want you to know, brothers, that what has happened to me has really served to advance the gospel" (Phil. 1:12). Then, after talking about the betrayal and the rivalry of ministry, Paul says that whether Christ is preached in pretense or truth, he is preached. That is enough for him and he rejoices.

How do you move from being hurt to rejoicing? The answer is, you take up your cross. That is not an easy answer, but it is necessary.

This is what Christ commanded us to do when he said that we must take up our cross: "If anyone would come after me, let him deny himself and take up his cross and follow me. For whoever would save his life will lose it, but whoever loses his life for my sake will find it" (Matt. 16:24–25; see also Mark 8:34 and Luke 9:23–24).

The hurt person who is not embracing his pain as a means for God to do something in his life is the person who is stuck and for whom the clock has stopped. He is not denying himself. In fact, the very thing he wants to do is feed his pain: they hurt me, they said this about me, and I was offended. But Jesus says, "Take up your cross; follow me; deny yourself. Whoever seeks to save his life will lose it, but whoever loses his life for my sake will find it."

We want to think about bearing a cross as enduring physical pain, and it is. We want to think about taking up our cross as standing up for truth and maybe taking some hits for it, maybe even being a martyr for it. Throughout church history many have done so. But the context of the cross is betrayal. The context of the cross is the pain of being hurt by those close to us.

Zechariah 13:6 speaks of "the wounds I received in the house of my friends." This is the painful life of which the people who came to my office were speaking. This is the pain you may feel in your heart. This may be where you are living today.

Sadly, some people live by the words of the late playwright Tennessee Williams, who wrote, "We have to distrust each other. It is our only defense against betrayal."[2] God does not call us to live in distrust, but to live by faith in Christ. It is not that I implicitly trust all men; it is that I trust God in all situations. And this makes life sweet.

Recently, I heard about a friend from my past who had moved to a new city. I asked where he was going to church and was told that he was not going anywhere. He speaks of past betrayals, past pain in churches, and says that he will not allow himself to be hurt again. He distrusts. It is now his defense against betrayal. His ten-year-old son related his philosophy of life. What a lesson he is getting.

God does not want that to be your lesson. Rather, the lesson is that you and I are called to take up our cross in every way, including our relationships. It is true that you may be hurt. But you are a disciple of one who was betrayed, who was hurt, and you are not above Jesus.

To follow Christ is to embrace the cross, to say with the Bible, "Although he was a son, he learned obedience through what he suffered" (Heb. 5:8). We are not gluttons for punishment. We are not masochistic and desirous of pain. We are followers of Christ, and to identify with Christ, we bring all of our heartache to him. We find meaning in our suffering, even in our betrayals, through Christ.

In dealing with the experience of being hurt by others, taking up the cross is to stop being a victim and to begin being a victor through Jesus Christ.

Now think about what God is teaching victims in Genesis 50:

> But Joseph said to them, "Do not fear, for am I in the place of God? As for you, you meant evil against me, but God meant it for good, to bring it about that many people should be kept alive, as they are today." (Gen. 50:19–20)

Here we can identify our second step. If the first step in moving from victim to victor in our painful relationships is to take up our cross, the second is to take off our crown.

2. Take off your crown.

Stop pretending you are sovereign and confess the truth that only God is sovereign. J. C. Ryle wrote, "Of all the doctrines of the Bible, none is so offensive to human nature as the doctrine of God's sovereignty."[3]

I have found this to be true in my life. It is the final act of submission—to say that I am not in control, but God is. In confessing this, you will find healing.

If you are in control, then your crucifixion has no meaning. You are holding hostage in your heart that person who is perpetrating this injustice upon you. You cannot forgive because you have been wronged.

If God is sovereign, then the one who brought your cross to you is Christ himself. This is hard language.

It means that like Joseph, like Paul, and, yes, most like Jesus, you see God himself sovereignly ruling in all of life to bring you to the point of crucifixion. Crucifixion is, as Gene Edwards puts it, meant to destroy.[4] God has destruction on his mind in your life. He intends to purge, to refine. The old Puritan Thomas Watson wrote that we are to put the gold into the fire until the last dross has drained from the metal. Jesus was crucified by his Father. And it was to his Father that Jesus cried.

In my counseling session with these three families, things got very still at this point—even uncomfortable. Maybe it is so with you right now. But Joseph escaped being a victim and became a victor by naming God, not as the author of evil, but as the one who caused it to work together for good. Paul was not bitter against the Jews. Instead he prayed for them and said that he would give his life for them, even though they had betrayed him. He suffered and ultimately lost his life because of their condemnation of him. Why? Because God was in control of Paul's crucifixion. God, not man, is in control.

Here is how Matthew Henry sums up the fact of the sovereignty of God and the painful and even sinful things that are sent to us: "God often brings good out of evil, and promotes the designs of His providence even by the sins of men; not that He is the author of sin, far be it from us to think so; but His infinite wisdom so overrules events, that the issue, that ends in his praise [was at first] to His dishonor as [in] the putting of Christ to death."[5] We need to learn to say with Jonathan Edwards, "Absolute sovereignty is what I love to ascribe to God. It has often been my delight to approach God, and adore him as a sovereign God, and ask sovereign mercy of him."[6]

At a conference I attended, I listened intently to a pastor. He spoke about his struggles with applying God's sovereignty to his own life. He said that there was a time when his wife put a sticky note on the bathroom mirror that said, "When will you stop trying to be the general manager of the world?"

Ouch. Do you try to be the general managers of the world too? As one recovering controller to another, you know there is only one. And that is good news. Because the crucial step in coming to terms with any pain that has come against us, including getting hurt by someone close to us, is to say, "God, you are in control. What do you want me to learn?" We need to let God deal with those who have hurt us. It focuses our pain, not on those who have hurt us, but on the God who has led us to our own Calvary. Malcolm Muggeridge once put it this way: "Every happening, great and small, is a parable whereby God speaks to us, and the art of life is to get the message."[7]

Grasping God's sovereignty—not as a theological concept, but as an act of utter submission and child-like faith—will move you from being a victim to being a victor.

We have taken note of two steps: take it to the cross; take off your crown. But it all comes together in the third step.

3. Go to your Gethsemane.

Paul says that he wants to identify his sufferings with Christ so "that by any means possible I may attain the resurrection from the dead" (Phil. 3:11). Recognizing that God sent his imprisonment in order to cause him to know Christ's resurrection was a crucial step for Paul. Recognizing that his brothers' awful act of treachery was under the sovereign control of God was a moment of faith for Joseph.

Gethsemane is the place where you—like Jesus, like Paul, like Joseph—come face-to-face with your crucifixion and with the fact that God is in control. Note that if there is to be a resurrection—a new life to emerge from the pain, the betrayal, the hurtful words—then there must be a crucifixion. And if there is to be a crucifixion—by the Father for the good of many—then there must be a Gethsemane moment when you say, "Not my will but yours be done." There must be a moment when you say, even when the shadow of pain is falling over you, "They meant it for evil, but God meant it for good."

This Gethsemane—your Gethsemane, the moment when you respond to the pain you have received from others—is the turning point. You will either go forward as a walking wounded, who is destined to carry the burden for years, or you will accept the trial as coming from God and open your life to him. If you take up your cross and take off your crown, your response of faith will lead you to total trust in the Lord and his will for your life, total forgiveness of others and release of them to the Lord for his will in their lives, and total freedom for you and his wonderful grace being unleashed as a powerful reality.

This is what I told the friends who came to see me that day. It is what I want you to know, because we all will be hurt. We are all a bunch of recovering sinners living with each other. Like family members, we say things that hurt, and we make mistakes that hurt others and ourselves. We live in a world that is fallen and where we are always being victimized by someone or something. But the Lord calls us to identify our sufferings with Christ, so that we become like him through the things that come against us.

I want to share something with you. I don't say it to bring attention to myself, but to show God's faithfulness. There was a time in my ministry when some situations brought pain. I cannot give you details about those times, for they are too painful to me and too personal for others. As I was hurt, I brooded over my pain. I did not see this truth. I was unforgiving in my heart toward those people and toward one man in particular. The pain festered for a long time. I would say, "This man has hurt me and ruined something good for me." I hope by now that you see I was wrong. There is no resurrection for those who suffer without Gethsemane submission. There is no new life. There is only the grave. But if that is your story, it does not have to end that way. There is always a Gethsemane moment available for you. For me, I found my Gethsemane in a hotel room when no one else was watching. I said, "Lord, you did this. Not that man. Not those people. You did this. And shall I not drink this cup?" I had lost much. I cried and I cried. The tomb opened. I rose and lived again.

One day, many years later, I again saw the shadow of a cross coming over me. This time, I remembered. I came home to my wife and said, "The Lord has called us to the field of testing. We have entered the time of the cross." The crucifixion came. I felt moments when the Father had abandoned me.

But by then I knew, He had abandoned his Son, my Lord, so that he would never abandon me. I knew from my lesson in the cross that to embrace the thing that was to come against me was to release and forgive those who may have seemed to bring the hammer and the nails and the cross, for it was God who would do this. As one writer has put it: "Love . . . ordains every struggle to strengthen us, lights every furnace to purify us, mingles every bitter cup to heal us."[8] I have never known God's love more than when I took up the cross, took off the crown, and went to my own Gethsemane.

I gave this testimony to these three families, and I saw God moving to bring new life. It didn't take years of counseling. It took one moment of saying, "I want to know him and the power of his resurrection in my life. I want to take up my cross and follow him, to claim him as sovereign King even in my rejection and my betrayals." I watched faces lift up from prayers of confession to joyful release, years of pent-up pain dripping away and new life, like fresh sunshine, shining through.

God will do it for you, too. If you have been hurt, wounded, abandoned, sinned against, or betrayed, God will transform you from a victim to a victor as you trust in the one who was hurt, wounded, abandoned, sinned against, and betrayed, but who pronounced forgiveness from the cross. Jesus Christ has transformed the cross from an instrument of destruction sent by the Father to an instrument of salvation ordained by God. In him there can be no more victims—only victors.

Will you say, "I want to know him and the power of his resurrection, and share in his sufferings, becoming like him in his death, that by any means possible I may rise again?"

Will you believe that though "they" meant it for evil, God meant it for good? Will you go on and live this risen life that Christ offers you?

Questions for Reflection

1. Have you (or has someone you know) been hurt by another Christian? If so, how was your faith affected? What about your relationship with your church?

2. The pain of friendly fire can "stop the clock" in a life. How is life lived once the clock is stopped? What is the key to restarting the clock?

3. How did Joseph make sense of the pain he experienced by the hand of his brothers (Gen. 15:15–21)? Does this help you as you process your own painful experience? Why or why not?

4. Does "embracing the pain" that comes our way require us to be gluttons for punishment? How would you describe a healthy, biblical way to embrace pain?

5. The first step in moving from being the victim of a betrayal to being victorious in the face of betrayal is to take up your cross. What does that mean? What are the indications that you have moved from victim to victor? What is a sign that you haven't done so yet?

6. Tennessee Williams wrote, "We have to distrust each other. It is our only defense against betrayal." Do you agree, or is there another defense against betrayal as we live in relationships with people who are as flawed as we are ourselves? Can you rewrite the first sentence in that quote to change it from a sadly negative philosophy into a hopeful and biblical one?

7. Is the following statement true or false? "We must implicitly trust everyone in order to live a life of

faith." If it is false, what one word would you change to make it true?

8. Reflect for a moment on the ten-year-old boy who related his father's philosophy of life that was developed as a defense against betrayal. Who in your life is watching? Does what they see lead them in the footsteps of faith?

9. J. C. Ryle wrote, "Of all the doctrines of the Bible, none is so offensive to human nature as the doctrine of sovereignty." What do you think he meant by this, and do you agree or disagree?

10. How can healing from betrayal be found in confessing that we are not in control? What is the first step in loosening the grip of control that our heart has on the one who wronged us?

11. Taking up your cross and embracing pain are part and parcel of crucifixion—a process that Gene Edwards says is meant to destroy. How can crucifixion and destruction be instruments of good in your life?

12. If someone close to you betrays you, confessing that God is in control and asking him, "What do you want me to learn?" can refocus your heart. Do you agree or disagree, and why?

13. In Gethsemane, Jesus came face-to-face with crucifixion and submitted to God's will that he endure it. How did Jesus ready himself to submit? How does that apply to the way we respond to pain suffered at the hand of others?

14. Explain the difference between forgiving and forgetting betrayal and releasing the one who betrayed you to God's will for his or her life. Are you able to see how the former option could

minimalize the offense, while the latter is more honest and could result in freedom for you?

15. If love "ordains every struggle to strengthen us, lights every furnace to purify us, mingles every bitter cup to heal us," are you able to see God loving you in the midst of your situation? If not, pray that the Holy Spirit would bring you to a place where you are able to thank God and worship him in spirit and in truth—even in your pain.

11

OH, MY SON!

2 Samuel 18:33; 23:5; John 16:33

Heart Cry

The cry of the heart of the man of God is not only a cry for a cause, but also a cry of pain and hope in the midst of pain.

After the rebellion of his third son, Absalom, David was told that his son had been killed in battle at Ephraim Wood. And thus we read these words in the inerrant, infallible Word of the living God: "And the king was deeply moved and went up to the chamber over the gate and wept. And as he went, he said, 'O my son Absalom, my son, my son Absalom! Would I had died instead of you, O Absalom, my son, my son!'" (2 Sam. 18:33).

And I add to these words the final cry of David as he lay dying: "For does not my house stand so with God? For he has made with me an everlasting covenant, ordered in all things and secure. For will he not cause to prosper all my help and my desire?" (2 Sam. 23:5).

Finally, as Christ faced the cross, he gave divine words of healing to his disciples that we claim as well: "I have said these things to you, that in me you may have peace. In the world you will have tribulation. But take heart; I have overcome the world" (John 16:33).

Between the bitter cry of "O my son" and the believing confession of "He has made with me an everlasting covenant" lies the truth of our own pain and our own hope. Here is my prayer:

> Dear Lord, we have heard the cry of courage from David. Now we hear the cry of pain. How we are reminded that you, O Christ, cried out from the cross to your Father and ours. How we remember and cherish the thought that you came to live as a man to know our pains, and not only to identify with us, but to die for us on the cross. Come now, we pray, and minister to us. Come, O Christ, and turn our cry of pain to a prayer of dependence and in time to a cry of praise. In your name, O Christ, I pray. Amen.

William Faulkner and King David

Speaking at a men's retreat in Mississippi, I said, "I must say that William Faulkner is an acquired taste." Thomas N. Walters, a professor of English at North Carolina State University, might have put it best when he wrote:

> All too often Faulkner's name merely evokes in high school students visions of confused sentence structure, depraved characters, despairing darkness, grotesqueness, etc. On the other hand, his warm, generous characters, his broodingly loving

descriptions of the land, his storytelling ability, and above all, his humor are too often overlooked.[1]

Now you may be wondering why I bring up Faulkner. Here is why. I always try to read an author whose works have explored the past, the people and the soul of the place where I preach. I read Thomas Wolfe for North Carolina. I read Steinbeck before I go to Monterey or even Oklahoma. I read Walker Percy about Louisiana. But I read Faulkner on Mississippi. While he can be difficult, he also used Mississippi to explore the human condition. And Faulkner once wrote, "There is no such thing as was—only is. If was existed, there would be no grief or sorrow."[2]

Now that statement may be as enigmatic or complex as some of his novels, but I like it. It gets at what we are dealing with here. William Faulkner was saying that there is no "was" in terms of making mistakes and enduring heartaches. It is always in the present state. "There is nothing new under the sun" is another way to put it, and in speaking of the pain of fathers and men in general, this is true. The characters, in their sins and their pains, as well as in their hopes, are not just things of the past. It is now. No "was." Just "is."

The great Oxford, Mississippi, author wrote a book based on the biblical story of David's son, called *Absalom, Absalom!*[3] It is an extraordinarily complex tale of a poor man from Virginia, Thomas Sutpen, who marries a wealthy woman from Mississippi. Through the backdrop of Mississippi and the Civil War, fortunes won and lost, sin, shame, and four generations of heartache and degradation, Faulkner tells a complex tale about the legacy of this dysfunctional family. Through these generations Faulkner seems to be telling the story of the complicated life of the South that he sought to understand himself. The biblical story of David's family life, which led to the horrible scene with Absalom, may not be quite as complex as Faulkner's book, but it comes close. It is a complex story, despairingly dark, but there is also hope.

Absalom was the third son of King David. David had many wives, but this son came from his marriage to the daughter of the king of Geshur. To get at just how complex the situation was, we need to read about the wives and children of David in 1 Chronicles 3:

> These are the sons of David who were born to him in Hebron: the firstborn, Amnon, by Ahinoam the Jezreelite; the second, Daniel, by Abigail the Carmelite, the third, Absalom, whose mother was Maacah, the daughter of Talmai, king of Geshur; the fourth, Adonijah, whose mother was Haggith; the fifth, Shephatiah, by Abital; the sixth, Ithream, by his wife Eglah; six were born to him in Hebron, where he reigned for seven years and six months. And he reigned thirty-three years in Jerusalem. These were born to him in Jerusalem: Shimea, Shobab, Nathan and Solomon, four by Bath-shua, the daughter of Ammiel; then Ibhar, Elishama, Eliphelet, Nogah, Nepheg, Japhia, Elishama, Eliada, and Eliphelet, nine. All these were David's sons, besides the sons of the concubines, and Tamar was their sister. (1 Chron. 3:1–9; see also 2 Sam. 3:3)

This is where Faulkner got his complex stories! Well, this third son was called the most handsome lad in the whole kingdom (2 Sam. 14:25). But David's sin of taking wives, not to mention his murderous plot to kill his loyal military leader, Uriah the Hittite, in order to marry his wife, Bathsheba, led to the fulfillment of God's word that violence would not leave David's house. And indeed Amnon, David's eldest son, fell into sin as he raped Tamar, the full sister of Absalom. David's negligence in doing nothing about this sin by his eldest son enraged the third son. So Absalom did something. He murdered Amnon to avenge his sister's shame. He was banished from Israel to live with his maternal grandfather in Geshur. After three years, he was brought back home, but it took another two years for Absalom to face his father. The root of bitterness in Absalom strangled his respect for his father. With his superstar status, good looks, and charismatic persona, and desiring his own kingdom, Absalom mounted a popular rebellion against his father.

Ironically, David began his career by running from King Saul, and he found himself again on the run, this time from his own son. But the tragedy came to a climax with the battle of Ephraim Wood. There, west of the Jordan, Absalom's army was decimated, and its leader, known for his good looks and long, flowing locks, was killed as his hair got caught in a low-hanging limb. The prince hung there alive until Joab killed him. David had warned his men to deal gently with his son. But his army had little patience for this rebel. And so he is told. Thus we hear the cry of the heart of this man of God: "O my son Absalom, my son, my son Absalom! Would I had died instead of you, O Absalom, my son, my son!" (2 Sam. 18:33).

William S. Plumer, a nineteenth-century American pastor, took this cry and applied it to the fathers and mothers in his congregation and wrote: "Beware how you teach and guide and act and speak in regard to your child, lest by God's judgment he die in his sins, and you, like David, cry when it is too late: 'O my son Absalom! my son, my son Absalom! Would God I had died for thee, O Absalom, my son, my son!'"[4]

There is great biblical warning here, and we need to hear it. But we also need to find the way, the way to hope and healing. So we will see in this passage that God knows the pain of a broken man, and that he gives his promise to the believing man.

God Knows the Pain of a Broken Man

I begin again with Faulkner's observation that not much changes in terms of sorrow in this life. What happened to David might not happen exactly to us, though I suspect there are those who have deep wounds that were touched by the mere reading of the story.

Patrick Morley writes that he has observed that men are not doing well in our society.[5] He has found three things:

Men are tired. They are exhausted from the pace of life—emotionally, physically, relationally, morally, and financially. Men are being called upon to spend quality time with their wife and children, work harder at the office or plant, serve God in their church, be a good citizen and a good neighbor, keep their yard clean, have a satisfying career, and spend time with God and alone. It is tiring just reading what we are expected to do!

Men feel that something isn't right. There is a growing sense of despondency and clinical depression among men. Our fathers could fight a war, build a suburban dream, and create the American dream, but we are not even sure what our roles are after the feminist revolution. What is a man?

Men who are Christians are often committed to values, but not to Christ. Men are giving time and energy to programs and ministries on boards, committees, and even mission trips, but their understanding of Jesus Christ alive within them is often lacking.

And thus, as these fathers and husbands struggle with these issues, their families flounder. And sometimes they hit the shoals and get wrecked by the temptations of this present evil age. We think instantly, and sadly, of Tiger Woods or even our former president, Bill Clinton, and the pain that can come because of sins of the husband or the father. Because men are the heads of their homes, their sins affect all the members of their household in a deep and profound way. And sometimes they are left crying the cry of David over Absalom.

The Bible does not hide the pain of David or its source. But the Word of God does not say more about it than that. There is no divine piling on. It is enough that he sinned, that he was warned of the consequences of such sin, and that those horrible consequences came. Jesus and others in the New Testament treat David as a biblical hero. He is remembered for his faithfulness. But that faithfulness must be seen in the context of his pain and brokenness in this cry from his heart.

There are three parts to this cry that I want us to consider.

1. In David's cry there is a cry of searing loss.

He lost one of his sons. Maybe you have a heart that is hurting because of the loss of a son or daughter through death. It doesn't have to be the kind of loss that David encountered for us to cry out to God in pain. Just last week, our community was faced with the loss of a young woman who was the daughter of faithful missionaries to Taiwan. Her father grieved and cried out to God for the loss of his beautiful daughter. Perhaps your heart is breaking from the loss of someone in your family. Maybe that loss is through death. Maybe that loss is through the pain of a prodigal child. Maybe that loss is through distance. But God is with you. He will never leave you nor forsake you. And the very thing that causes you to cry out to God is the thing that brings you close to the heart of God. Hear the cry of David in his loss:

> When the righteous cry for help, the LORD hears
>   and delivers them out of all their troubles.
> The LORD is near to the brokenhearted
>   and saves the crushed in spirit.
>
> Many are the afflictions of the righteous,
>   but the LORD delivers him out of them all.
>   (Ps. 34:17–19)

Let this word bring comfort to your cries. The gospel of Jesus Christ does not deny our crosses, but transforms them, sanctifying our sorrows, so that we find comfort from the Lord in the very things that hurt us.

2. In David's cry there is a cry of mournful regret.

David cries the cry of a man who wishes that he could go back and change the clock. If only he had not

210

taken more than one wife! If only he had repented of that and sought to bring peace to his family! If only he had not plotted the murder of Uriah! If only he had intervened, as a parent, to deal with the horrible situation with Tamar and Amnon and to quiet the heart of Absalom. "If only, if only . . ." These are the saddest words in the English language. "If only I had reared my children in the faith . . ." "If only my walk had matched my talk, then maybe . . ." "If only I had seen the horrible consequences of that one moment of flirtation . . ."

But I thank God that Brit Hume was right when he said that only the Christian religion offers redemption. He took a lot of heat for saying that, but that news commentator was a good biblical commentator at that point! For in Jesus Christ there is hope. You do not have to live in the "if onlys" of life. You are not a victim, but a victor in Christ. Yes, there are consequences, but there is forgiveness in Jesus Christ.

I once heard Billy Graham on *Larry King Live*. He was asked if he had any regrets in life. I wonder if Larry King thought that Billy Graham would say, "No, I have lived for the Lord and I have no regrets." In fact, the other guest on the program, a non-Christian religious leader, was asked the same question and he had said that he had none. But Dr. Graham said that he had many. He was a sinner, and thus regretted his sins and how they had hurt him, but especially how they had hurt others. In fact, he said he most regretted the time away from his children. But he said that he had to leave his regrets with Christ, who not only forgives but also renews.

One of my favorite verses in the Bible is Joel 2:25, "I will restore to you the years that the swarming locust has eaten, the hopper, the destroyer, and the cutter, my great army, which I sent among you" (Joel 2:25). I thank God that Christ has come to take the "if onlys" of our lives and change them to "I will restore." I thank God that your regrets can be taken and left at the cross. Maybe you need to do that now.

3. In David's cry there is a cry of longing.

David would have preferred his death to that of his son. Men like to fix things. We would prefer that any pain in our children's lives come to us. This is a cry of longing.

It is a cry that we must take to David's greater Son, Jesus, who also cried, "My God, my God, why have you forsaken Me?" It was a cry that Christ heard, for "the righteous cry out and he hears them and delivers them." It was a cry that the last book of the Old Testament tells us is answered by Jesus Christ. For we read of one coming who will bind up the pain of fathers and the generations after them: "And he will turn the hearts of fathers to their children and the hearts of children to their fathers" (Mal. 4:6).

I believe that even in this mournful cry of David we have gospel hope. Listen to Matthew Henry's commentary on this verse, and let it seep into your soul: "But while we learn from this example to watch and pray against sinful indulgence, or neglect of our children, may we not, in David, perceive a shadow of the Saviour's love, who wept over, prayed for, and even suffered death for mankind, though vile rebels and enemies."[6]

Let your longing be quieted by our weeping Lord, who stands in your place, who forgives all who come to him, and who restores the lost causes through the cross.

212

God Gives His Promise to the Believing Man

David goes from a cry of pain over his son to looking forward to his greater Son. And we read the final words of David: "For does not my house stand so with God? For he has made with me an everlasting covenant, ordered in all things and secure. For will he not cause to prosper all my help and my desire?" (2 Sam. 23:5).

This is a promise that David's house, ruined by his sin, would be restored by God's covenant promises. He recognizes that God was at work, even in his pain and his brokenness, to bring about his purposes. David's life was no lost cause. And thus we must depart from Faulkner's dark and complicated stories of family dysfunction to the sunlit uplands of God's promise to David. Through David came our Savior, Jesus Christ.

Many years ago I was a prodigal child. I was an orphan. I had no mother or father. My Aunt Eva reared me just a few miles across the border from Mississippi. And my life as a child was as complicated, it seems, as a Faulkner novel. Sin and shame brought me into this world. And the great questions of life haunted me. Though reared by a godly woman, I took my questions and left home. On my journey, I went far from God. In those days I lost much, including my three deaf children. I would not see those children for many years. I do not need to share the sordid details of what brought that about, but it cut my soul to the quick. I was a broken man in every way.

When I married Mae, she began to pray, and she went back to college in Kansas to get a degree in deaf communication. She graduated with highest honors. After that she became the interpreter for D. James

Kennedy on the *Coral Ridge Hour*. But that is not why she continued to sign. My wife believed that one day I would be reunited with those children and she would be there to "sign" our reunion. My Aunt Eva believed even as she aged into her 90s. My pastor, Robert Baxter of Olathe, Kansas, also believed and he prayed every day.

When John Michael was born, we were greatly blessed. But we continued to pray to see those three children again. I was such a broken man that I would often run away in public places where children were— run away to weep—because I could not stand the pain of seeing little ones, knowing that there were children out there that I could not see. I cried the cry of loss, of regret, and of longing. I cried the cry of David in my own way.

Indeed, as I had become a follower of Jesus, I knew I had to take this pain to Christ and I did. I set up an appointment with Christ to go to him every Friday night and lay my burdens before him. I cried out and claimed his promises to me. God gave me faith, for I lacked any in myself. My faith was emboldened by my wife and Aunt Eva and Pastor Bob. Then, when my Aunt died, a man came up to me in the funeral home and told me that he knew where those children were.

To make a long, complex, Faulkner-like story a little shorter, I want to tell you that Mae "signed" a reunion with each of those children who were at Gallaudet University. And God brought reunion. Pastor Bob praised the Lord for answered prayer. My wife praised the Lord. And Aunt Eva, now in heaven worshipping Christ face-to-face, had her earthly prayers answered.

So God is restoring the years the locusts ate. My life is not perfect. But my Savior is taking the broken pieces and fashioning a new man in Christ. He is still at work. And I have found that the very thing that caused me to cry out in pain has caused me to cry out the promises of God and to cling to Calvary in the midst of the storms of life.

Like David, you and I can claim the covenant promises of God. Our pain is shaped by his promises to hear prayer. And our prayers become providence. And providence leads to praise.

Let me ask you now: where does this passage touch you the most? Where is the pain? Is it a wife who left you? Is it indeed a prodigal son? Is it your own sin or a sin committed against you? Everyone has pain. But every believer has a promise—the promise of a Redeemer.

God the Father had to give up his only Son to win back his creation. But from the shame and the pain of the cross in the stark, cold, dark stillness of the tomb burst forth the promise of new life in the resurrection of Jesus Christ. This was what David looked to. This was the covenant blessing he sought as he left this world. And this is the covenant blessing we seek in our lives.

Jesus is alive. Everything has changed. Hear these words with the joy of the hymnist who wrote "Jesus, Jesus, Jesus, Sweetest Name I Know":

> All my life was wrecked by sin and strife,
> Discord filled my heart with pain;
> Jesus swept across the broken strings,
> Stirred the slumbering chords again.[7]

David cried out against all loss, regret, and longing, even as death came to his door, "for he has made with

215

me an everlasting covenant." Will you now claim this covenant of grace in David's greater Son, Jesus Christ, the living God who creates all things anew? Will you now receive him by faith for the first time—or maybe for this time?

Hear your Savior speak to you: "I have said these things to you, that in me you may have peace. In the world you will have tribulation. But take heart; I have overcome the world" (John 16:33). Let us cry out to God from hearts of faith.

Questions for Reflection

1. William Faulkner said, "There is no such thing as was—only is. If was existed, there would be no grief or sorrow." What do you think he meant by this as it relates to our mistakes and heartaches? Do you agree or disagree, and why?

2. David neglected to deal with the sin of his son Amnon against the sister of his other son, Absalom. Negligence on the part of the father led to the rage, murder, banishment, and bitterness of the son. Who did God hold responsible for sin, and was that fair? Has bitterness ever strangled or threatened to strangle a relationship that is important to you?

3. It has been said that we often fall, not because of our weaknesses, but because of our strengths. What were some of Absalom's strengths and blessings in life? How did these eventually work against him? Can you think of some modern-day examples of people whose strengths became weaknesses and led them to calamity?

4. What was your reaction as you read Patrick Morley's observations about men today being tired, feeling something isn't right, and being committed to values but not to Christ? If you are a man, did any of these three shoes fit? If you are a woman, did any of these observations describe a man you know and love? What effect do you see on the family of the man you have in mind? What effect do you see on the man?

5. "The gospel of Jesus Christ does not deny our crosses, but transforms them, sanctifying our sorrows." If an ordinary cup of wine or juice and bread are sanctified—set apart from common to holy use—in a Communion service, how can sorrow and pain be sanctified? Can you give an example from your own life or the life of someone else?

6. What does it mean to live in the "if onlys" of life? Does a relationship with Jesus erase the consequences of those situations you wish you could do over? If not, how can real regret coexist with real hope in Christ? (Read Joel 2:25 again.)

7. Matthew Henry suggests that parents engage in watchful prayer against sinful indulgence as well as neglect of their children. Gross neglect is easy to describe, but what are some examples of neglect that is more difficult to see but still endangers the souls/lives of children? We are charged with providing for our children, but what constitutes indulgence? What makes it sinful?

8. Between the painful loss of the author's deaf children and the joyful reunion many years later, Mae gives a wonderful example of putting faith and

hope into practice while waiting on the Lord. What did she do that "put shoe leather" on her faith in God's ability to restore? Think of your own situation of loss or that of someone you love. How might Mae's example translate even now—while you are straining to see just a glimmer of hope on the horizon? How does this type of waiting on God glorify him?

PART 6

PAIN AND PRAISE IN FUTURE HOPE

12

OVERCOMING THE OBSTACLES OF LIFE

Joshua 1:9; 5:13–15; 6:1–5, 20, 26–27

This passage also teaches that nothing is more effectual to produce confidence than when trusting to the call and the command of God, and feeling fully assured of it in our own conscience, we follow whithersoever he is pleased to lead.
—*John Calvin*[1]

How Do You Deal with Obstacles in Your Way?

How do you deal with the obstacles in your life? I learned about how to face obstacles when I played football in high school. One time I was running the ball back from a kickoff. I broke through the first wave of defenders and was running full speed down the field with only two defenders left, and one of them was the kicker. Now I was big at that age, and these guys were not. But they were obstacles between that goal line and me. I thought, "I can run around these obstacles, or I can run through them." I decided to run through them. They grabbed hold of my jersey, and then together jumped on my back. I kept limping toward the goal line with those two gangly guys on my back! Then they lost their grip on my shoulder pads and began to slide down my back. But they were not letting go! They grabbed onto my hip pads, and my hip pads began to slide down my legs. Finally I made it into the end zone, but I didn't have any pants on! I never figured out why the entire stadium was laughing and the cheerleaders were running away as I pressed on to the goal!

The lesson that I learned then was that the way you deal with the obstacles in your life may reveal the most personal things about you. Now that was funny—at least to me as I think back on it now.

But I wonder how you are dealing with the obstacles in your life. Obstacles include things like difficulties in your work, in your relationships, in your health, in your heart, and with your faith.

There is a place in God's Word where a man named Joshua, the leader of Israel, had to learn how to deal with obstacles. He had led his people over the Jordan River. The land of milk and honey now lay before them. But in between the Promised Land before them and the wilderness behind them was an impregnable fortress called Jericho. We agree completely with Marten H. Woudstra: "The story of the fall of Jericho . . . must not be treated as a mere product of Israel's faith. It is, we believe, historical narrative as well as 'theological' presentation."[2] This seemingly impregnable city was built centuries before Joshua was ever born. It was a mighty fortress with walls twenty-five feet high at some places and over six feet deep.[3] It was the very symbol of Canaanite invincibility.

Now we all know what happened from our Sunday school song: "Joshua fit the battle of Jericho . . . and the walls come a-tumblin' down." But do we know that when the walls came down, God's lessons for our lives came pouring forth? Here we see a faith-defining victory that shows us how obstacles are overcome in our lives.

Follow the progression of this passage, and just as Israel marched seven times on the seventh day, so here are seven steps to seeing God unleashed against the obstacles in your life:

1. Follow the leader (the leader, Joshua, falls before the angel of the Lord).

Much misunderstanding persists on why the people of God were called by God to go into Canaan to wage war. Most of the criticism of the Bible's bloody past is tied to these battles of Joshua. But God had commanded it because of the obscene sinfulness and wickedness of those who had rejected faith in God and were polluting the land, killing their own children, and permitting the worse sorts of sin. Israel's conquest of the land, beginning with Jericho, was also the instrument of God's judgment against these pagan city-states.[4]

The story of this conquest begins, not with a leader rising up, but with a leader falling down. In Joshua 5:13–15, Joshua, the successor to Moses, encounters one who identifies himself as "the commander of the army of the LORD."[5] Hearing that, Joshua falls on his face before him. He then instructs Joshua, "Take off your sandals from your feet, for the place where you are standing is holy." We heard this when God appeared to Moses in the burning bush. This "commander of the army of the Lord" is not identified as an angel. Rather, the divine writer calls him, in Joshua 6:2, "the Lord." I must agree with the great old commentator, Matthew Henry, when he says: "This Man was the Son of God, the eternal Word. Joshua gave him Divine honours: he received them, which a created angel would not have done, and he is called Jehovah, chap. 6:2. To Abraham he appeared as a traveller; to Joshua as a man of war. Christ will be to his people what their faith needs."[6]

Praise God! What do you need God to be for you today? What does your faith, to quote Matthew Henry, "need"? Peter needed restoration after having blasphemed and denied the Savior and having run away from Calvary. So Christ came to him, to give him what his faith needed.[7] Jesus came to forgive him and recommission him to feed his sheep. When Paul felt all alone after having preached in a synagogue, where he was "opposed and reviled" (Acts 18:6), Jesus assured him that he was there when others were against him:

> And the Lord said to Paul one night in a vision, "Do not be afraid, but go on speaking and do not be silent, for I am with you, and no one will attack you to harm you, for I have many in this city who are my people." (Acts 18:9–10)

To each of the seven churches in the book of Revelation,[8] suffering from trials coming from within and without, the Redeemer came to meet their respective needs—seven times, seven churches, seven problems, and seven solutions! What do you need from the Lord? Let me put it this way: what obstacle do you need God to defeat, so that his name will be glorified and his daughter or son will be satisfied? He is the God who told Joshua, when he was called to be a leader, "Have I not commanded you? Be strong and courageous. Do not be frightened, and do not be dismayed, for the LORD your God is with you wherever you go" (Josh. 1:9). So before Joshua went into battle, the Son of God came to him to encourage him. Before you go anywhere, follow the Leader.

One time, when I was in school, our football team was on the bus, going to play a team that was way out in the country. Now since we were way out in the country ourselves, this trip was off the map altogether. The poor old bus driver, who was a volunteer dad, was getting all kinds of help—and by that I mean backseat drivers—telling him, "Turn at this turnip patch up here," "I think we should have turned back there at that country store," and so forth. Finally, he pulled that bus over, put the brake on, got up, turned around, and said, "We've got too many drivers on this bus. Now, who wants to drive?"

The question before each of us is, who is going to drive the bus? In the book of Joshua, the leader is not Joshua. It is the Lord. The question is going to be, who is the captain in the battles you face? The question of your life is, who is going to be your Leader?

2. Trust in the victory.

In Joshua 5:10 we read: "While the people of Israel were encamped at Gilgal, they kept the Passover on the fourteenth day of the month on the plains of Jericho."

Joshua would not allow the Israelites to miss the victory celebration, even though they had not yet overcome Jericho. This is one of the most faith-filled, moving pictures in the Bible. The desert is finally behind them, the Promised Land lies in front of them, but the plains of Jericho are in between. And what do they do? They celebrate the Passover. They remember the redemption of God in Egypt before facing the enemy at Jericho.

That is not a bad way to live. In fact, each time we celebrate Communion in our church, we are keeping the covenant feast "on the plains of Jericho."

I am an Army Reserve chaplain. A bad back has kept me out of the theater of war. So I teach chaplains and support the war effort at our installations here at home. But I have talked to chaplains and other soldiers who have related to me the power of Communion in war. It would be an otherwise insane act, except for the cross of Christ. The chaplain gathers the squad at midnight for Communion before they go out on patrol in the caves of Afghanistan. They are celebrating God's redemption before going into the battle that could take their lives. But the chaplains tell me, "I never knew the power of the Lord's Table until I looked into the eyes of soldiers who didn't know if that would be their final hour of life."

I love to read the optimistic preaching of James Stewart. In "Christ and Human Need" the great master preacher of Edinburgh wrote about how Jesus ministered to the villages through which he passed:

> Here in the Gospel it all worked out so gloriously! There was no disappointing of those eager hopes. "Whithersoever He entered, as many as touched Him were made whole." And in those village homes that

night, the joy!—can you imagine it?—since Christ
had passed that way. The lights burned late in many
a cottage window; and psalms of David—often sung
before—went rising up to God that night with a new
note of lyrical gratitude and elation.[9]

In Passover then and in Communion now, and in worship right where you are reading these words, there
can be celebration before "the plains of Jericho."

How will you celebrate? You center your celebration, as Israel did, in the redemptive work of God. That
redemption came to its fullness for humanity in the
cross of Christ. Are you willing to step out now and
trust in Christ's victory even as you face your Jericho,
your citadel of opposition? Jesus Christ welcomes you
to himself on the plains of your Jericho. What is your
Jericho? Are you willing to name it? Are you willing
to trust the gospel truth that John taught us? "Little
children, you are from God and have overcome them,
for he who is in you is greater than he who is in the
world" (1 John 4:4).

3. Believe the promise.

Jericho would not fall as a result of the way that
armies normally conduct warfare. There would be
no massive buildup of armies, no flanking moves, no
surprise attacks at dawn. Rather, the people of God
were to follow a divine prescription that was based on
a series of sevens and that recognized the importance
of the ark of the covenant (the sign of God's presence
with Israel) and a cry of deliverance. All of this, without going into it, represented a call to faith for God's
people to overcome the obstacle of Jericho in God's
way so that he alone would get the glory.

Unbelievers have put forward some ridiculous thoughts that the collective marching around the city loosened the fortification of bricks and that the sudden shout on the seventh day did the final damage. Rubbish! The walls came tumbling down because of God's salvation, apart from man's contribution!

It was a mistake when Jefferson Davis made Leonidas Polk, an Episcopal bishop, one of his generals in the Civil War, and it would be a mistake to put a chaplain in command of an artillery battalion in a war today. It made no sense to put priests on the front line with the ark of the covenant, except that it would give all the glory of victory to God!

In this first great victory it had to be made clear to Joshua and to Israel: God made the promise, and he would secure the promise. He would not share his glory with man.

Now this leads us to see that Israel not only believed, but obeyed! This is the fourth step toward overcoming the obstacles of life.

4. Obey the plan.

Joshua 6:20 is the glorious statement of obedience: "So the people shouted, and the trumpets were blown. As soon as the people heard the sound of the trumpet, the people shouted a great shout, and the wall fell down flat, so that the people went up into the city, every man straight before him, and they captured the city."

What an amazing portrait of God's conquest over sin! "The description is dramatic, recalling similar moments in the description of the crossing" (e.g., verses 3, 14, 16).[10] What an amazing portrait of how God would also defeat every other enemy of the Lord through his appointed captain! "The symbolical nature of Jericho's fall, historical though it be, should not escape the reader. The very first city of the Promised Land was to be Israel's by a mere shout raised at the command of Joshua, the Lord's servant."[11]

Obedience to the captain of the battle, Joshua, brought conquest. Obedience to the captain of our struggles, the new Joshua, our Lord Jesus, likewise brings conquest over the original sin that stands like this pagan fortress. But just as the original sin fell, so every other sin must fall through the whole of our journey, until at last we reach our heavenly home.

You see, there is a plan afoot in the world! It is that you shall be saved without the help of a man. You shall be saved in only one way, and that is through our Lord and Savior Jesus Christ. Through him and his death on the cross, a most unlikely way to secure salvation, you will know eternal life.

Yet there must be obedience. It is repentance and faith in Jesus alone for eternal life. And it is trusting God in the same way over and over again throughout all of your life.

When you consider the Jericho that you may be facing in your life, it is only through God in prayer that you will succeed in surmounting that obstacle. This is not passivity. It is hard work to follow the Lord and tough spiritual labor to trust in God as you face the fortifications of hardship: "Trust and obey, for there's no other way, to be happy in Jesus, but to trust and obey."[12]

Next comes the fifth of the seven steps that bring conquest. I want to back up and think through verse 20: "The people went up into the city, every man straight before him, and they captured the city."

5. Watch God work!

The plan worked! When you follow God's plan, his way, the walls of the obstacles you face will fall, one way or the other.

Now let me pause right here. We read that Elisha, God's prophet in 2 Kings, told Naaman, a pagan army commander who had leprosy, to bathe seven times in the Jordan and be healed. And when he did so, he was healed. Similarly, Jesus went into the room where Jairus's dead twelve-year-old daughter lay and said, "Little girl, arise!" She got up and began to walk. Yet when the nails of a Roman soldier were hammered into the Son of God, he was not healed. When men mocked the one who made them and gambled for his clothes, the angels did not break in and stop it. And when Jesus cried out, "My God! My God! Why have you forsaken me?" there was no response from heaven, even though the earth shook and the daylight receded into gloomy darkness to cover the awful sight.

But God was at work! For through the cross, God's Son tasted death. And from that death came resurrection for Jesus and resurrection hope for all who put their trust in him.

You may be assured that God is still working, even though your prayers are not being answered in the way you suppose they should be. God will surely bring victory, though you cannot see it now. You may rest, for God is at work, if you:

- Follow the leader—Jesus Christ
- Name the obstacle—your sin
- Believe the promise—of salvation and hope in Jesus

- Obey the plan—by repenting and turning to him, or leaving your burden with him in prayer

I want to encourage you with William Cowper's words:

> God moves in a mysterious way
> His wonders to perform;
> He plants his footsteps in the sea,
> And rides upon the storm.
>
> Ye fearful saints, fresh courage take;
> The clouds ye so much dread
> Are big with mercy, and shall break
> In blessings on your head.[13]

Now if you have this down, go on to number six.

6. Leave it alone!

In verse 26 we read that Joshua gave a curse that Jericho must never be rebuilt. This teaches us that when God has defeated our foe, we should not go looking for it again. This is not just, "Don't go sin again," but "Don't doubt God's victory." When God saves you, you need not go back there again. It is finished. And when God overcomes the obstacles in your life, you don't go through life as a victim of what once oppressed you. It is over. You are more than a conqueror through the very thing that was once your obstacle.

Finally, we come to the last step.

7. Live the promise.

> So the LORD was with Joshua, and his fame was in all the land. (6:27)

Trusting in God leads to a new way of life. The one who appeared to him, and the one that Joshua followed, led him all the way to victory. Knowing that Jericho was defeated gave strength to Joshua, and the word spread about his leadership.

I have told you about my Aunt Eva. Businessmen and laborers alike would go to her to inquire of the Lord about their lives, for the Lord was with her and his hand guided her. Everyone in our little community respected Aunt Eva because she knew the Lord.

I love to tell the couples who come to see me that I believe in a God who can help them. I believe in a God who can overcome all of their obstacles to give them new life. And I like to tell them that, based upon God's Word, I also believe that one day I am going to have to call upon them to help counsel another marriage in trouble. In the midst of their own troubles, some may have a hard time believing that. But I tell you it is true. You see, when God works victory, and destroys Jericho, you know his presence in a new way. And others, with their own Jerichos to conquer, come to see what God has done in your life.

In a Company of Heroes

The late Stephen Ambrose wrote a fine book on fathers and sons that he called *Comrades*. There is a line in this book in which a boy asks his grandfather, a World War II veteran, "Grandpa, were you a hero in the war?" "No," he answered, "but I served in a company of heroes."[14]

One of those heroes came from along the banks of the Tennessee River in a little Kentucky community called Turkey Creek. One night nineteen-year-old Ed sat with his dad next to a Silvertone radio listening to the voice of Walter Winchell. It seemed that the Imperial Japanese Army was about to storm the beaches of California. This farm boy was convinced that he had to go protect his country. He told his dad, "I'm going to join the Marines and fight." He had no idea what lay in store for him. Before Ed went to boot camp, he went to church. And one Sunday night in Murray, Kentucky, that young man stayed behind in his pew after everyone else had left. The pastor came over and sat down with him. And Ed, deeply guilty, placed his faith in the finished work of Jesus Christ. He writes about what happened: "It was on that day that God forgave me of my sins and I experienced the miracle of new birth in Christ. As my burden of sin was finally laid at the foot of the cross, my heart was filled with joy and relief. I thought to myself, 'Now I am ready for war, because now I am ready for eternity.'"[15]

Ed Harrell went through boot camp and sea school and was assigned to the USS Indianapolis. On the night of July 30, 1945, only weeks before the war ended, the commander of the Japanese submarine I-58 put the Indianapolis in his periscope crosshairs and shouted a command to fire. In less than fifteen minutes, Ed and 899 other men of the ship's 1,196-man crew were swimming in an oil slick in the shark-infested cold waters of the Philippine Sea. Their heavy cruiser was at the bottom of that sea. In four days the 900 survivors became 317, as sharks, hypothermia, and dehydration depleted the ranks. Ed Harrell was one of two marines swimming in that sea those four days. And when his buddy, blinded by the oil and saltwater, delusional from thirst and saltwater poisoning, tried to slip away, Ed told him, "There are two marines in this ocean today and there will be two marines pulled out of this ocean whenever they come. You are not going anywhere!" So Ed held prayer meetings in the Philippine Sea. Ed writes in his book, *Out of the Depths*: "As the terrors of night surrounded me, my heart ran frequently to the Lord in prayer. The indwelling Holy Spirit would help me think of Scripture. When this would happen, I would lay hold of His promises and pray them back to Him with an attitude of awe and great joy."[16]

On the third day, when thirst was overwhelming, Ed held a prayer meeting and pleaded for water. They watched as a cloud formed in the distance, floated over them and rained down wet mercy. They were amazed as a pallet of rotten potatoes floated by them, and they "feasted" on the filth, but it gave them enough sustenance to last.

They were finally rescued. Ed Harrell now tells of God being with him in the deep and signs his books with Psalm 27:1, "The LORD is my light and my salvation; whom shall I fear? The LORD is the stronghold of my life; of whom shall I be afraid?" But Ed's strength, and how he rallied others to be saved during that great obstacle of life, started with a teenage boy giving Jesus Christ his heart in that little Kentucky chapel.

It always starts like that. It always starts with the visitation of the Lord, who said, "Come unto me . . ."

I don't know what you may be facing tomorrow. But I know the One who is here today.

Joshua defeated Jericho because the Lord was with him to accomplish it, and that victory began a march through a land that Israel would eventually claim. Jesus Christ defeated the greatest obstacle of all—death and hell—when he went to the cross for sinners. He offers eternal life and abundant life to those who turn from self and receive him by faith. Come and claim your land that God has set before you.

What is the first obstacle in your life that must fall? What is your Jericho?

Questions for Reflection

1. The author once learned a serious lesson in a most amusing manner on a high school football field. Looking back, he said, "The lesson that I learned then was that the way you deal with the obstacles in your life may reveal the most personal things about you." Do you think that the way we deal with obstacles builds character or reveals character?

2. Referring to the theophany—or appearance of God—to Joshua (Josh. 5:13–15), Matthew Henry writes, "To Abraham he appeared as a traveller; to Joshua as a man of war. Christ will be to his people what their faith needs." Are you facing an obstacle right now that seems insurmountable? How would you describe what your faith needs Christ to be for you?

3. Footnote 8 highlights Jesus' different messages to the churches at Smyrna and Laodicea. Does what we think our faith needs always match what Jesus thinks our faith needs? Can you give an example from your life when you prayed and didn't receive what you asked for, but, in

retrospect, received what your faith and growth in character needed?

4. Joshua led the people of Israel in a celebration of the Passover, remembering how God redeemed them in Egypt, even as they faced a new enemy at Jericho. Can you name a past victory won by God for you? Take a moment to celebrate it now in gratitude and worship, even as you face a new obstacle.

5. Joshua and company marched, shouted, and blew trumpets as evidence of their belief in God's promise and provision. Is there something that you can do, or stop doing, that would make it evident that you believe in God's ability to provide you with victory over the obstacle you are facing?

6. Do you agree that facing obstacles in trust through prayer is not a passive pursuit, but hard spiritual labor? Why or why not? Would you say that you are currently laboring in prayer over something?

7. If you are following Christ, naming the obstacle within yourself, hoping for deliverance with confidence in Christ, and turning to him in prayer with your burden, are you able to rest as you wait on God? Why do you think we find it so difficult to "rest" in faith?

8. "When God saves you, you need not go back there again. It is finished. And when God overcomes the obstacles in your life, you don't go through life as a victim of what once oppressed you." This is true, but is it your experience? If not, ask God to grant you the faith to live in the light of his victory—or in his sure promise of it.

9. Do you know someone who has experienced God's victory over an obstacle and, thus, has come to know his presence in a new, deeper way? Would you consider going to that one with your "Jericho" and asking him or her to pray for you? Then ask God to give you the sacred privilege of helping someone in the same manner one day—and faith to trust that he will.

13

GOD'S MESSAGE TO SPIRITUAL AMPUTEES

Mark 9:42–50

The church is a hospital for sinners, not a
museum for saints. So we should expect
that many Christians' lives would not
compare well to those of the nonreligious
(just as the health of people in the hospital
is comparatively worse than people visiting
museums).
—*Tim Keller*[1]

A Radical Remedy

The battlefields of the American Civil War were some of the worst places imaginable. Military tactics had not kept up with military weaponry. When the .58 caliber minie ball hit the bone of a soldier, it expanded and crushed and shattered the bone. Of the wounds recorded in the Civil War, more than 70 percent were

239

to the extremities. And so, amputation was the common operation of the Civil War surgeon. Civil War doctors were called "Sawbones" for slang. I quote from a medical history of the Civil War:

> The field hospital was hell on earth. The surgeon would stand over the operating table for hours without a let up. Men screamed in delirium, calling for loved ones, while others lay pale and quiet with the effect of shock. Only the division's best surgeons did the operating and they were called "operators". Already, they were performing a crude system of triage. The ones wounded through the head, belly, or chest were left to one side because they would most likely die. This may sound somewhat cruel or heartless, but it allowed the doctors to not waste precious time and to save those that could be saved with prompt attention. This meant that common battlefield surgery was the amputation.[2]

It was hard. But amputations saved lives.

Amputation is a chilling thought unless your very life depends on such a radical remedy for your disease or your wound.

Some of us are going to need amputation. The Great Physician, Jesus Christ, is the doctor who orders this extreme procedure.

The Bible teaches us that we are engaged in spiritual warfare.[3] In this warfare, we must not, through our own sin, lead others into sin. In the solemn teaching of Jesus recorded in Mark 9:42–50, we learn what awful judgment awaits those who lead others into sin. Kent Hughes sees this as particularly pointed to those in ministry. He calls this "a terrifying statement of ministerial responsibility."[4] It is, in fact, a sobering message for all believers to beware of the hypocritical, egotistical use of power that could derail the faith of other believers.[5] In this passage the Lord commends radical surgery to prune our lives of the sins that would destroy others along with us. This is what I mean when I speak of spiritual amputation.

There are four critical questions I want to pose as we consider this passage, and I pray that the Holy Spirit will conduct his surgery on you and on me.

The first question is this:

1. What is spiritual amputation?

In speaking of amputation, it may seem to you that the language is extreme. But listen to the language of Jesus in Mark 9:45–47.

> And if your hand causes you to sin, cut it off. It is better for you to enter life crippled than with two hands to go to hell, to the unquenchable fire. And if your foot causes you to sin, cut it off. It is better for you to enter life lame than with two feet to be thrown into hell. And if your eye causes you to sin, tear it out. It is better for you to enter the kingdom of God with one eye than with two eyes to be thrown into hell. (Mark 9:43–47)

This is extreme language. As Geoff Grogan writes, "If [it seems to be extreme] this is surely what He intended, because the justification for such language lies in the awfulness of the prospect of eternal punishment."[6]

The logic of this passage leads us to ask questions of ourselves:

- Are there things I am doing with my hands, hidden activities or habits, which possess me?

Would they bring disrepute on the name of Jesus and become a stumbling block to others?

- Are there places where my feet are carrying me that I have no business being, maybe a social establishment, or an association, or a place of entertainment that would undermine my testimony and lead another astray?

- And what of my eyes? In an age like ours, with pornography available twenty-four hours a day, seven days a week, in the privacy of our homes, are there things I gaze upon that, if anyone knew about it, would bring embarrassment? Or worse, would this bring shame to the name of Jesus?[7]

The truth is that our senses are always slaves to what our hearts desire. If our hearts desire Christ and his love, our senses will be ruled by that desire. If our hearts are unregenerate, they will desire sin.

What does your heart desire?

There have been, in church history, some who have sought to be so pious as to take this literally. They have cut off their limbs in order not to sin. This became so widespread that the Council of Nicaea had to outlaw the practice. But the language of Jesus is hyperbole and metaphorical. It is the heart that inspires the limbs to sin. It is thus spiritual, not physical. Spiritual amputation is a radical response to the gangrene of sin in our lives that causes other believers to fall into sin. This divine surgery is only accomplished through the work of the Holy Spirit in our lives causing us to love Jesus more than our sin. It requires us to put sin to death in our members.

The Word of God deals with the presence of flesh-
liness in God's people. It has always been a source of
great danger. When Israel was in the wilderness, and
Moses was on the mountain getting the law of God,
Aaron remained with the people. But they refused to
follow the revealed pattern of worship and drew Aaron
into the worship of a golden calf—a profane, pagan
worship style of Egypt.

Each of us must be careful in our own lives and
daily bring our heart before Christ to mortify the sin
that remains.

Jesus said, "It is the Spirit who gives life; the flesh
is of no avail. The words that I have spoken to you are
spirit and life" (John 6:63).

Paul wrote, "I have been crucified with Christ. It is
no longer I who live, but Christ who lives in me. And
the life I now live in the flesh I live by faith in the Son of
God, who loved me and gave himself for me" (Gal. 2:20).
And Paul warned the Romans: "For if you live according
to the flesh you will die, but if by the Spirit you put to
death the deeds of the body, you will live" (Rom. 8:13).
And then the Colossians: "Put to death therefore what is
earthly in you: sexual immorality, impurity, passion, evil
desire, and covetousness, which is idolatry" (Col. 3:5).

A. W. Pink wrote about this: "Nothing short of the
complete denying of self, the abandoning of the dear-
est idol, the forsaking of the most cherished sinful
course—figuratively represented under the cutting off
of a right hand and the plucking out of a right eye—is
what He claims from every one who would have true
communion with Him."[8]

If you desire to have true communion with Jesus,
there will have to be spiritual amputation in your life.

243

It happens when we see God for who he is, our sins for what they are—an offense to a holy God—and we see how our sins infect others. We must come to the point where we love the pleasure of freedom from sin more than we love the passing pleasures of sin. It is when we hate our sins and love the blood of Jesus shed for our sins that we cry out to him, "Lord, save me." At that moment, the Spirit of God moves into your life and saws off the infected parts of your life that are keeping you from God. Crucifixion is painful. And spiritual amputation involves a radical severing of sin from our lives.

Are you prepared to follow Jesus and embrace this life of death to self and living to Christ? We must see that Jesus is speaking to his disciples to beware of sin. He is speaking to us today.

The second critical question of the passage is this:

2. Why is spiritual amputation required?

Here is the answer when our profession of faith is out of step with our testimony to Christ: "Whoever causes one of these little ones who believe in me to sin, it would be better for him if a great millstone were hung around his neck and he were thrown into the sea" (Mark 9:42).

Spiritual amputation is required because our sin can cause childlike believers to stumble. The little ones here include not only children but also any who are weaker. Geoffrey Grogan, along with others, wonders if the child was the son of Peter, for they were in a home in Capernaum. Peter had a believing wife (1 Cor. 9:5), and so he may have been pointing to this child who had come to faith through the ministry of his parents.[9] But we really don't have to go that far. Jesus used the child simply as an example of a disciple who is not great. Anyone who was not part of the Twelve was a little one. Paul wrote about such when he wrote:

> Live in harmony with one another. Do not be haughty, but associate with the lowly. Never be conceited. (Rom. 12:16)

> We who are strong have an obligation to bear with the failings of the weak, and not to please ourselves. (Rom. 15:1)

In John Calvin's day, he was concerned about the Roman Catholic priests who were not receiving the teaching of the gospel of grace. He was also concerned about the common man who was not allowed to have access to God's Word. This was John Wycliffe's concern. He wanted the common Englishman to know God's Word. They were the little ones in his life. And the little ones in our day surely include our children. But the expression also includes Christians who have not been well grounded in God's Word. It includes those who are not being fed the Word. It includes the disabled who need our love. It includes Christians in places where the Spirit is moving and they need our help, lest they become discouraged. It means reaching into the people groups who are entering our nation and need our ministry. These are the little ones.

Now, we are told that the gangrene of our sin can cause those who are weaker to sin. Some translations say, "cause to stumble." One says that through our sin

245

we become a stumbling block to these little ones. The Greek word is *skandalizo*. It is a verb that is causative. It means that the sinful actions of believers can cause someone to fall into temptation and to actually sin. Now they are not here acquitted of their sin because of this. But, like an accomplice to a felony is also responsible, Jesus is saying that those who cause others to sin are culpable before the Lord.

In the text, the disciples could have caused the child to sin by marginalizing him as unimportant. In the same way, by forbidding the man casting out demons to minister, they could have thrown cold water on his efforts. Perhaps he would say, "Well if I am not a part of the Twelve, I am of no use to God. I will go back to my old life of sin. This Jesus really doesn't need me and thus doesn't care for me."

In our lives, we can cause others to sin in the same way. Christians and churches that don't show God's love to the least of people bring disrepute upon the name of Jesus. Christians and churches who don't care for the disabled believer, who put children and youth on the back burner, who don't seek to minister to the poor, who boast of their wealth and power while people are suffering from injustice or hunger or oppression, cause those believers to fall into sin. Men who boast of their faith in Jesus and then leave their families and cause their children to doubt God's love, are putting a stumbling block into their lives. Think of all the little children whose concept of Christ is marred by an unloving father or an abusive parent or an ungodly mother. Think of the wives who cannot relate to God because of the harshness of their husbands. Think of parishioners who cannot see the love of Jesus because of the judgmental attitude of their pastor. God have mercy. May God cause all of us to see the wickedness of this sin, how pervasive it is, and how awful it is in the eyes of a holy Redeemer who gave his life for sinners.

Spiritual amputation is required because the consequences of not dealing with the spiritual disease and of infecting others are awful.

And this leads us to our next critical question of the passage.

3. What if spiritual amputation is not administered?

The question is put as we read these words in verses 47–49:

> It is better for you to enter the kingdom of God with one eye than with two eyes to be thrown into hell, 'where their worm does not die and the fire is not quenched.' For everyone will be salted with fire. (Mark 9:47–49)

Jesus is teaching us that hell is the result of not dealing with the gangrene of sin in our lives. No one taught more on hell than Jesus Christ. Yet we tend to speak of it infrequently. And in modern dialogue about Christianity, we may even feel it is better to neglect the doctrine. I agree with Spurgeon when he said:

> Our dear Redeemer, whose lips are as lilies dropping sweet-smelling myrrh, in great tenderness of heart warned men of the sure result of their sins; and none used stronger or more alarming language than he did concerning the future of ungodly men. He knew nothing of that pretended sympathy which will rather let men perish than warn them against perishing.

Such tenderness is merely selfishness excusing itself from a distasteful duty.[10]

In Ezekiel 33:6, the Lord warns those who excuse themselves from the duty of warning others of hell: "If the watchman sees the sword coming and does not blow the trumpet, so that the people are not warned, and the sword comes and takes any one of them, that person is taken away in his iniquity, but his blood I will require at the watchman's hand." There is a heaven and there is hell, a place of eternal torment. It is reserved for those whose sins are not forgiven by faith in Jesus Christ. And our Lord says it is reserved for those who would call themselves his disciples and yet lead little ones, little children in the faith, astray from Jesus. We have seen what this means. And thus, without repentance, this sort of spirit reveals a heart that is not in touch with God's grace. It reveals a haughty, high-browed, self-boasting spirit that is antithetical to the true state of a sinner saved by grace. And thus we should, if we have led others astray by a critical spirit, by self-boasting, or by an elitist attitude, be driven this day to ask if we are God's own children. We should quickly turn to Jesus and see that it is by grace alone that we are saved by faith in the finished work of Jesus on the cross. Then, with our hearts filled with gratitude to Christ, we are able to seek to build up the lambs of Jesus and not to hurt them by our hypocrisy.

This leads me to the last part of this passage, which deals with the fruit of a renewed heart and mind towards the Lord in these matters. And so I pose this last critical question with regard to the text:

4. What will be the positive effect of such a radical spiritual surgery?

I ask this question as we look at this part of the passage: "Salt is good, but if the salt has lost its saltiness, how will you make it salty again? Have salt in yourselves, and be at peace with one another" (Mark 9:50).

Jesus was teaching in a Galilean fishing village. Salt would have been readily available for preserving fish and for Jesus to use as a recognizable illustration. This illustration was also used by the Lord in the Sermon on the Mount in Matthew 5:13, when Jesus said, "You are the salt of the earth."

Our Lord, in using the illustration of the salt with its savory and preservative properties, is speaking of his disciples. They are the salt. But if they are no longer salty, no longer filled with the taste of grace and truth and a heart for others, how can they be salty again? The answer from the Word of God is that with man it is impossible, but with God it is possible. The question is put by the Lord to provoke us to introspection, to confession, to the awareness of our ridiculous clinging to self and works and prestige and power, so that we will rely on the grace of Jesus Christ. Then Jesus tells us, "Have salt in yourselves, and be at peace with one another." Jesus is referring to his disciples' argument about who is the greatest. He has in mind their sectarian spirit, which caused them to rebuke and restrain a man ministering in Jesus' name. He has in mind the need for radical spiritual surgery, an amputation of gangrenous parts, in order for them to live. They will have salt at the table in their fellowship, and peace will be the rule. They will then be able to move from such pettiness, which is hurting the little ones, to a world of people who are lost and who need Jesus. Their eyes will be lifted to the harvest. Their lives will be seasoned with grace.

Is your life seasoned by God's grace in Jesus Christ? Do you feel the burden of your sin that could cause another believer to stumble? Does it cause you shame in your Master's presence? Then, quickly, turn to him. Turn with me to find our hope.

This age desperately needs salty saints who refuse to rot like the unpreserved fish of Capernaum, which ruined not only themselves but other fish as well.

Sooner or Later I'm Running

I admit this is a hard passage for us to hear. But radical surgery is needed for a radical disease. We are soldiers in a time of war. The hard teachings of the Lord for his own disciples were necessary if they were going to follow him in the war zone of their day. We are in spiritual warfare, according to the Bible, and we also need this teaching.

Staff Sgt. Dan Metzdorf is thankful for his amputation. It saved his life. It was January 27, 2004. Sgt. Metzdorf was ten days into his deployment with the Army's elite 82nd Airborne. He was about fifty miles south of Baghdad, when on routine patrol his vehicle was attacked as he was trying to clear a roadway. "I felt myself hit the ground," Metzdorf said. "Then, all the pain sets in. And it hurt so badly—I couldn't feel my right foot, but it was still attached to me. That's the only part I couldn't feel, but everything else was so much pain."

The damage to his leg was so extensive that it had to be amputated. His wife, Teresa, was notified, and she had to make the phone call to Dan's mom. It was hard. And after months of rehab at Walter Reed Medical Center in Washington, D.C., Dan saw that his amputation not only saved his life, but it strengthened him. He refused to be discharged from the Army. He fought the case and won.

Dan Metzdorf refused to feel sorry for himself. "It's just a miracle by God that I'm still alive," he said. "You know, it's a huge thing that happened to me, but it's not that bad," he chuckled. "You know, some people have bad hair days, I have bad leg days."

This past year, he competed in the New York City Marathon. And now Sgt. Dan wants to return to Iraq. And here is what got me. He said, "[You focus on that missing leg every minute] 'cuz every time I take a step, you have to think of your step every time. . . . Right now, I'm kind of like a baby at it, and I'm just kind of crawling, but sooner or later . . . I hope I'm running."[11]

The strength of that sergeant is in his weakness. But his new strength is helping him to run the race.

How will we run the race?

You know, the church is like a marathon of amputees all limping together and leaning on Jesus to get through. But the amazing thing is that this is what is so attractive to the other cripples. They do not see themselves, but their Savior in them, when they lean on him. That is the message of the passage.

That is the invitation today: to see your sin, to turn from it, and to embrace others in the same condition. But that is not all. Now show them the One who enables spiritual amputees to run—and to run with power and with grace.

Questions for Reflection

We begin with three hard questions from the chapter that require a hard look at our hearts:

1. Are there things you are doing with your hands, hidden activities or habits, which control you? Would these things bring disrepute to the name of Jesus? Could they become a stumbling block to others?
2. Are there places you are going where you have no business being? Do you frequent a social establishment or place of entertainment, or have an association, that would undermine your testimony or lead someone astray?
3. Are there things on which you are gazing that, if discovered, would cause embarrassment? Would being found out bring shame to the name of Jesus?
4. If our senses are always slaves to what our heart desires, what do your answers to the above three questions reveal about the desires of your heart? Take time to think deeply and carefully about this as Psalm 51:6 NIV says of God, "Surely you desire truth in the inner parts; you teach me wisdom in the inmost place." Ask God for wisdom and mercy. Read Psalm 37:4. Ask God to make his desires yours.
5. When the Scriptures use the battlefield language of spiritual amputation, the solemn words of warning are directed to the disciples. Can you name

some otherwise wholesome desires common to followers of Jesus that, taken to an extreme, might tip toward idolatry and require spiritual surgery?

6. If the New Testament words "little ones" do not always mean children, describe the type of people to whom it might refer. Who within your circle of influence might be considered as such and why? (See Rom. 12:16 and 15:1.)

7. If gangrene is defined as "death and decay of tissue in a part of the body due to lack of blood supply, injury, or disease," describe some causes of spiritual gangrene in the body of Christ. Describe some of the effects.

8. Charles Spurgeon warns against "a pretended sympathy, which will rather let men perish than warn them against perishing." Read Jesus' conversation with a woman caught in adultery and note his balance of compassion and truth, warning and love (John 8:1–11). Have you had occasion to seek this balance of truth and love when warning someone against sin? If so, what was the result in their relationship with you? With God?

9. Since salt has both savory and preservative properties, list a few indicators of lost "saltiness." Consider how you are engaged in both respects as "the salt of [your appointed time and corner of] the earth." (See Acts 17:26.)

14

THE GRAND NARRATIVE

Exodus 1:1—22; 2:1—10; John 5:31—47;
Hebrews 1:1—4

Introduction to the Reading

Faith journey. Faith community. Chicken soup for the soul.

Our society has become very interested in spirituality in recent years. Go to any of the major bookstores across America where the swirling aroma of coffee sipped by people sitting in oversized leather sofas goes perfectly with selections from the spirituality section. Yet at the same time, as one modern observer puts it, we have lost our story, the narrative for our lives. As a result words, once clear and tied to a larger story and to propositional truths, have lost their meaning. Philip Yancey writes:

> No society in history has attempted to live without a belief in the sacred, not until the modern West. Such a leap has consequences that we are only beginning to

recognize. We now live in a state of confusion about the big questions that have always engaged the human race, questions of meaning, purpose, and morality.[1]

I want us to look in a book of the Bible, which seeks to say, "We do have a sacred story tied to propositional truth that gives meaning and hope to our lives." This story is a grand narrative: a great story that begins with a people called the Hebrews, but ends up being a story that reaches to the ends of the earth, even to our lives today. I want us to consider the truth that in a world of smaller stories, the Bible teaches that there is one grand narrative that is big enough for every person in every age, including you.

Our text is found in Exodus 1:1–22; 2:1–10 and then in Hebrews 1:1–4.

Hot Dogs and Religion

You may not think that hot dogs and religion have anything in common, but that was the subject of a conversation I had with a lapsed Jew and a Buddhist while standing in line at Pink's Hot Dogs in Hollywood. Mae, John Michael, and I were in line, at ten o'clock at night, to get one of America's best hot dogs, according to a PBS special we had seen. I know this sounds petty to some of you, but to John Michael and me the search for the perfect hot dog has become something akin to the quest for the Holy Grail! Well, at any rate, Mae came along with us and there we were with about seventy-five other people waiting to get a hot dog at Pink's. We talked about Pink's with the interesting couple in front of us, and then the fellow asked what

I did. That changed the conversation. He then volunteered that he had, for some time, done solo vocal work at several Presbyterian churches in the Beverly Hills area. He also told me that he was a Jew, but had given up on that as well. He said that he was free from religion and the better for it. His girlfriend, though, was on a different kind of journey, and was now into Buddhism. "Whatever works," he said. Both of them seemed to have lost cohesive stories about the meaning of life. I shared the story of Jesus with them. The Jew was very interested, but his girlfriend interrupted us: "Chili or chili with cheese?" And that was that—until we bumped into each other again as I was reaching to get my change from the clerk, and some of my money fell into his chili dog. I knew that whatever I had said was now blown by my blunder. But he smiled and said, "Don't worry about it, Reverend, I think you just blessed my hot dog!" He cleaned up my dime and returned it to me, and then thanked me. I think he may have been considering that there is, indeed, something to the old, old story for his life.

Postmodernity and the Loss of a Cohesive Story and Meaning of Life

The truth is that we have lost our story. Sociologists, like the writer Neil Postman, and Christian professors, like Marva Dawn at Regent College, tell us that the horrors of the twentieth century, with the Holocaust, communism, and two world wars, caused many people to question the old frameworks and traditional answers to the deep questions of life. What emerged was something called postmodernity. In postmodern thought, which today dominates popular cultural thinking, the basic idea is simply "Whatever works for you is great." As Tim Keller, a PCA pastor in Manhattan and one of the keenest thinkers on this, states, the issue is not to get postmoderns to believe in something, but to get them to stop believing in everything.

Has postmodern thinking, the loss of story, the loss of a metanarrative, come to you? Without arguing the point, I would say that wherever TV has gone, that most pervasive conveyer of popular culture and ideas, a mark has been left. Our society's recent struggles over placing the Ten Commandments in our court-houses and the question of same-sex marriage are examples of this. Whether in our big cities or our small towns, in America, England, Germany, or almost any-where else in Western society, this rejection of older ideas, older stories, has left us with many stories and thus no one cohesive story. And stories are how we understand our lives, our hopes, our dreams, and our struggles.

Can "the Old, Old Story of Jesus and His Love" Compete in the Postmodern World?

In the nineteenth century Fanny Crosby wrote a hymn about "the old, old story of Jesus and his love." Today we say, "This is my story, this is my song, prais-ing my Savior all the day long." A good question might be, "Can the old, old story, the story of Jesus and his love, compete in a postmodern, post-Christian world?" Christian thinkers like C. S. Lewis, Francis Schaeffer, and even the novelist Walker Percy have all felt that the loss of the older Christian cultural umbrella over the West, which included things that were not biblical and that blurred the radical message of God's grace, might provide a new and better opportunity to witness to the truth of authentic Christianity. I think they are right. I also think that is the testimony of biblical history, and church history supports them.

Our society has lost its common story, its common language. Yet we can be more optimistic than ever. Why? Because the old, old story of Jesus and his love is the compelling story of cosmic history. But we need to tell it, and some of us need to become reacquainted with it and embrace it in all of its simple glory once again.

I call your attention to Exodus. The Greek translators of this book named it with their word for "coming out," which is truly its main theme. It relates how God established a nation, a people, in fulfillment of his promise to Abraham, and brought them into a land where they could carry out their destiny to worship and live freely. So the Latin title became *Liber Exodus*, from which our English title comes.

Exodus tells a great story, a grand narrative of God's salvation of Israel. Jesus said that it is about him. The book of Hebrews says that it is about him. And the rest of the Bible shows that this grand narrative, this great story of God's salvation, is about what God is doing in our lives. God is leading us on a journey of a lifetime, and there is a grand narrative in our lives, a story of God's love. I believe that today, in our lives, God is leading us to a new place, our destiny, a place to be free, and a place where freedom means that our souls find ultimate meaning by worshipping the God of the Bible.

There are three features to the story, as it begins in chapters 1 and 2, that help us to see how God's story becomes our story.

1. This is a story of pain.

> Now there arose a new king over Egypt, who did not know Joseph. (Ex. 1:8)

The story of God's salvation begins in Exodus with a story of pain. Pain had brought Joseph to Egypt, but God had miraculously intervened in Joseph's life and in the lives of his father and brothers. God had, through the king, protected and even prospered Joseph's family. But after 430 years the sons and daughters of Joseph's family multiplied to a great number. The old allegiances were gone. The history had been revised or forgotten, and a new king was on the throne. Historians tell us that these events probably unfolded in the so-called New Kingdom during the reign of Ramses II.[2]

Matthew Henry tells us that in Genesis God shows us how he formed the world, but in Exodus he shows us how he formed a nation for himself to show forth his praise. In Genesis we have a covenant made with Abraham, and now we see God beginning to fulfill that covenant. But the formation of a people and the fulfillment of a covenant begin with great pain.

There is the pain of being forgotten. There is the pain of being mistrusted for your own blessings. In verses 9–10, the new ruler is insecure because Israel has increased and multiplied. You would think that this would mean more workers, but in fact the king grew fearful of insurrection. His insecurity caused Israel to suffer the pain of what verse 14 calls "hard service." This led to the pain of infanticide. The king, in his madness, decided to literally "cull the herd" of his slaves by ordering the murder of infant boys. This is the story of pain.

Isn't this the story of our lives? They are filled with pain, but according to the Word of God pain, heartache, and adversity are the fertile fields in which God works his wonders.

I enjoy reading the stories of people. I read about the life of Harry Truman in David McCullough's award-winning biography. Truman was a man with a painful past of financial hardship and family struggle. I read the story of Robert E. Lee. His story was a story of pain, as his father, a Revolutionary War hero, abandoned his family when Lee was a child and led a profligate life of shame. I read the life of C. S. Lewis, of Walker Percy they were stories of lives lived against the backdrop of agonizing setbacks. I read the life of Abraham Lincoln, whose whole life was a story of pain, beginning with the loss of his mother, a poverty-stricken childhood, professional disgraces, bankruptcy, and personal losses at every turn. I read the story of his murderer, John Wilkes Booth, a man possessed by his father's infidelity, with his own demonic passions raging within him and a twisted desire to please his mother by being as famous as his actor-father. In each case, pain is the common thread in the lives of people. You don't go through this life without some hits. But the rest of the story is always about how you respond to the pain. What is behind the pain? Does the pain have any meaning? Where is the pain leading you?

What is your pain right now? All of us have difficulty and trials. It is the way of life. The Bible says

that God is at work in and through our pain. It says
that God is not absent from life, but, for those who cry
out to him, we have great promises: "I waited patiently
for the Lord; he inclined to me and heard my cry"
(Ps. 40:1).

Whether the pain in our lives is the pain that comes
from someone else, or the pain that comes from our
own sinful decisions, or just the pain of living in a
world of woe, the Bible says that we can go to God
with our pain.

2. This is a story of providence.

The insecure ruler of Egypt had a seemingly inge-
nious, though diabolical, plan to reduce the number of
Israelites. He ordered the Hebrew midwives to snuff out
the male infants. But we read this in Exodus 1:17, 20:

> But the midwives feared God and did not do as the
> king of Egypt commanded them, but let the male
> children live. . . . So God dealt well with the midwives.
> And the people multiplied and grew very strong.

The story of the birth of Israel is not only a story of
pain, but also a story of God's providence. God super-
naturally worked through the pain to bring salvation
and even might and strength out of weakness.

Providence is God's ultimate ruling and overrul-
ing of all things, of all events, working them together
according to his own will. In this passage, as throughout the Word of God, we see that it is God who promises, and that it is God who delivers.

Look back at your own life. Can you see how God
used people and events to work together to bring you
to him or to bring blessing to you or to strengthen you

when you needed it? Truly, he works all things together for the good of those who love him, for those called according to his purposes.

Now, I want to show that the story of pain, superintended by the story of providence, always leads to the story of promise.

3. This is a story of promise.

> When the child grew up, she brought him to Pharaoh's daughter, and be became her son. She named his name Moses, "Because," she said, "I drew him out of the water." (Ex. 2:10)

I wonder if Moses cried when he wrote this. This is the story of promise in his own life, as well as in the story of the church of Jesus Christ. God had promised the world that the Messiah would come to redeem mankind from the curse of sin (Gen. 3:15). God had chosen Abraham to become the conduit for the promise. Israel was to nurture this promise until the fullness of time had come for the Lord Jesus to appear in human history. But it always seemed to hang between pain and providence. The promise was always in jeopardy. And here we see again how God intervened. He used Moses to lead his people to the Promised Land. And Jesus said that Moses wrote of him, so Moses was a prophet who pointed to the true Israel, the true Messiah, the true and final Promised Land, and the ultimate liberation. But for a while the promise was being hunted down. For a while the promise floated in a basket in a crocodile-infested river—until God's providence brought together, perfectly, ironically, the daughter of Pharaoh and one of the children he sought to kill. And the promise was kept. The Lord employed the very thing that was being used to oppose his will to bring his purposes to pass.

This story is really the story of faith throughout all the history of the world. God has a plan to prosper, to bring faith, to bring healing, and the devil and his unwitting followers try to snuff it out. But in the end God wins and his people win.

When John was on the island of Patmos, where he had been exiled for his faith, Jesus showed him that this pattern has held true throughout world history. I quote from Eugene Peterson's paraphrase of Revelation 12 in *The Message*:

> When the Dragon saw he'd been thrown to earth, he went after the Woman who had given birth to the Man-Child. The Woman was given wings of a great eagle to fly to a place in the desert to be kept in safety and comfort. . . . Helpless with rage, the Dragon raged at the Woman, then went off to make war with the rest of her children, the children who keep God's commands and hold firm to the witness of Jesus.

We read over and over again that the Dragon's painful plots are always thwarted. In Egypt it was Pharaoh who was trying to kill off the people of the covenant, but God overcame him. In Persia another agent of Satan sought to destroy God's seed, but Haman's plot to kill faithful Mordecai and annihilate the Hebrew people was undone by Esther. Haman was hung on the gallows intended for Mordecai. In the life of King David, God overcame the plots of a madman named Saul. He overcame the rebellion of David's son, and, perhaps most miraculous of all, even overcame David's own sin and shame. On and on it goes until at last Jesus, the Promised One, is born, and we read about how King Herod sought the life of this infant king. But God saved his Son through Joseph's dream and by using the visiting Magi for cover. On the cross, which was to be the end of the story, Satan's plans were once again undone. The lifeless body of the Nazarene was infused with resurrection power from heaven, and death was conquered!

The story of the lives of those who follow Jesus is likewise the story of providence, of a loving God who will not be denied. He is intent on saving a fallen race through his only begotten Son.

And you can be sure of this: that which he has begun in you, he will complete in the day of Jesus Christ. Jesus is always victorious, and he will be victorious in history and in your life.

I believe that God's story touched the life of an unbelieving Jewish man in Hollywood. I know that Satan doesn't want faith to be born, but God is strong, and the things that Satan uses to devour faith are used by God to establish it.

I believe that God's story of love is stronger than the pain that came into my life. Although my own sin, the sin of the world, and the sins of others might seek to prevent it or destroy it, God will defend and keep my faith and me.

I believe that God's story has come to you:

- To the young man who wants to believe, but can't get past the pain of a broken family, Jesus' love is greater than that pain. You can trust in him. The story of your life is that you will be free through faith in Jesus.

- To the young woman who wants to believe, but is trapped by the pain of something that went horribly wrong in her childhood and has her in the grip of fear, Jesus' love will use even that incident to show you how much you need the Lord and how much he loves you.
- To the older couple who never had children, but who prayed for so long, your faith has been floating in a basket, subject to being snuffed out by heartache, but God's love has and will birth more blessings than you could ever imagine.
- To the young seeker, who thinks one story is as good as another—God's story comes to you and will not be denied. You have been on a journey, a journey of pain, but the providence of a loving God has brought you face-to-face with a promise. And that Promise is God in the flesh, God on the cross, God risen from the grave, God in the Spirit moving in your heart right now, inviting you to say: "This is my story, this is my song, praising my Savior all the day long."

The Story has come to you. And the Story became flesh and dwelt among us. By faith, receive him today and let the journey begin. It is a journey that will finally bring you to a new heavens and a new earth, a place of "no more tears, no more pain"—a land of milk and honey.

The journey begins today. Are you ready to go?

Questions for Reflection

1. Tim Keller says that the issue is not to get post-moderns to believe in something, but to get them to stop believing in everything. Is there a significant difference between believing in nothing and believing in everything? Please explain. Which would be more difficult for you to address?

2. Describe some elements in what was called "the older Christian cultural umbrella over the West" that were unbiblical and served to blur the radical message of God's grace in Christ. In contrast, how would you describe authentic Christianity?

3. We cannot go through life in this world without experiencing pain in myriad forms. Would having a "grand story"—into which your smaller story with all its pains and sorrows fits—make the pain easier to endure or overcome? Why or why not?

4. Providence is God's ultimate ruling and over-ruling of all things, of all events, working them together according to his purpose. This includes those painful things that come at the hands of others, that come from our own sinful decisions, and that result just from living in this world of woe. Give an example of each from your life, and tell how God has used it to strengthen and bless you.

5. God promised the world in Genesis 3:15 that redemption—the act of saving something or somebody from a declining, dilapidated, or corrupt

state and restoring it, him, or her—would surely come. Over the centuries he has used many as conduits for the promise—Abraham, the princess of Egypt, Moses, Esther, David, Joseph, the Magi, Jesus, John, Paul, and you. What are some tangible ways you can carry forward the promise of redemption in your life and in the lives of others?

Conclusion

MEDITATIONS ON ROSES, DANTE, AND PSALM 40

While Sick and Rocking on the Front Porch of the Rest Home for Confederate Soldiers

Pope John Paul II, Barbara Bush, and Olympiad are bursting forth in magnificent color before my very eyes. I am sitting on our front porch, feeling jealous of the hybrid roses in their first spring bloom. The effects of the winter pruning and Mill's Magic rose food are fantastic. I had pruned these hybrids down to their root after allowing the remaining chlorophyll from last year to settle back down into the unseen places where life began. The plants were cut back with severe grace and then given strong food to begin the seasonal passage to where they are this day: alive, strong, colorful, pleasing to the eye, helpful for the rest of the garden as they "do their bit" to tie it all together.

I am jealous of them because I feel anything but alive and strong and colorful. I am surely not pleasing to the eye. I just told my wife, who has now become my nurse, that I look and feel like an old man sitting on the front porch of the Rest Home for Confederate Soldiers. My khakis feel baggy, my eyes appear dark, and my countenance seems to be fixed on something, perhaps a foggy battle that happened long ago when I was younger. I *am* writing in this condition, so I guess I am not dead. I just feel like it. I have been diagnosed with *neurocardiogenic syncope*. This condition of low heart rate, loss of energy, and propensity to either faint or get close to it, apparently stalked me for years, with panther-like stealth, before suddenly leaping out of nowhere to maul me without mercy. Wounded and seeking recovery, I have read the words of the psalmist and understood them better than I ever have.

"May those who love your salvation say continually, 'Great is the LORD!' As for me, I am poor and needy, but the Lord takes thought for me" (Ps. 40:16–17). "I am poor and needy"—who, me? I, who could preach twelve sermons in a week, work on three books at a time, write an article, and "be there" for my son, my wife, and our students, am now needing a nap of three hours to get through a day? Oh yes, "I am poor and needy, but the Lord takes thought for me." I am jealous of Pope John Paul II and Barbara Bush, who pontificate with fragrant confidence and laugh in the North Carolina breeze with cultured elegance while I shrink from life like I am in a different season. And I am. I have not been this sick in my entire life. The attempts to regulate the condition have not yet succeeded. I suppose that I am being pruned. There is no Mill's Magic rose food to perk me up, though the physician has tried several cures. But if I am a man of faith, then whatever chlorophyll of authentic religion that is remaining will surely return to the root source of my life and strengthen my soul for whatever lies ahead. I don't want to sound like I am dying. I don't think I am. I just feel like it. And I must use this time, an out-of-season time, to rediscover the source of my faith in Christ.

During this time I am being humbled by a power that is greater than my will. I was scheduled to be at an important gathering with the leaders of our seminary. Yet I am grounded by the doctor. No flying. No driving for now. "Could we rewrite the script beginning at the place where I give the speech at the Hilton Hotel?" joked President Reagan, as he lay near death at the emergency room at George Washington University Hospital. And I say, "Could we rewrite the script beginning just before I got that fever on Christmas Eve?" But no, the gavel of providence has been pounded and the deed is done. The bullet seems to be lodged and must be removed. I cannot be with my colleagues now. I find it exhausting to imagine that, at this moment, I could even join in by telephone and participate in any kind of truly meaningful conversation. I can take three hours to write these words, with great difficulty, and then I will be ready for bed. "Grounded," I say. So what does one do?

My son, who is discovering himself and his gifts, and his freedom to question his old man at the age of seventeen, and who has been a kind and patient attendant to me as well, spoke to me: "Dad, we can thank God for our sicknesses too. Do you believe that?" He was kindly testing me, reminding me, and really encouraging me from the sermons he had heard from his father's lips about how "God sanctifies our sorrows."

My son was like Jesus asking Martha about the resurrection at the tomb of Lazarus: "Do you believe this?" Faith had to be affirmed before mystery then, and so it does now. I smiled and replied to my son, "I do." So I have set out, in my syncope-sick mind, to find out the meaning of my affirmation. I gather enough energy to rock in the chair on the front porch (how great are our small successes when we are beset by unyielding weaknesses) and turn again to Psalm 40, but I miss it and end up in Psalm 41 (all for the better): "The Lord sustains him on his sickbed; in his illness you restore him to full health" (41:3).

The answer is altogether clear and altogether mysterious. The answer is that the processes of life, dormancy, and rebirth are outside of my control. It is the Lord who oversees the severe grace of pruning. It is the work of the Lord, our covenant God, providing freely what he requires from me, and he is my only hope. I am where I am because of a fallen world inflicting its cruel vengeance upon my sinful flesh, so filled with the nature of Adam. Yet Christ, who has redeemed all of creation, is also using that which would destroy me to bring about a new leaf—and perhaps even a new bloom.

I have had time to read in this time. I ordinarily whiz with ease through three or four books a week, as well as endless e-mails and journal articles and newspapers. Now I read three or four lines a day and wonder at the structure of the sentences, as a child's curious eye might follow a single ant in an ant farm teeming with the little creatures. The blessing in the bane is that I now see nuances I likely missed in healthier days. It was so, just now, when I read Dante's *Paradiso* (I, 22–27):

O holy Power, if you but lend me of yourself
enough that I may show the merest shadow
of the blessed kingdom stamped within my mind,

you shall find me at the foot of your beloved tree,
crowning myself with the very leaves
of which my theme and you make me worthy.

Oh "blessed kingdom stamped within my mind," I have missed you before. Oh "beloved tree," how I have longed to return to that cross in the deepest part of my soul!

I thus content myself on our front porch, sickly before the resplendent hybrid roses, that there is a power at work within me so that I shall also bloom. I (and the doctors) expect that this illness slowing me down will be regulated and I will bloom forth again soon with renewed energy. Yet the out-of-season dormancy has led me to see that there shall come a most severe pruning of that which is seen in order to discover that which is unseen. I am saying that this condition is but a taste of a time known only to God, when I shall be gone from view in this world, yet shine like the sun in another. I am writing on the Wednesday after Easter, and so I cannot but thank this covenant God of Psalms 40 and 41 for the Mediator of a better covenant, our Lord Jesus Christ, who has risen from the grave, blooming out of season and thereby reordering the old seasons with new ones that have never been seen before. The "Eighth Day" is now my hope. So tired am I of this weakness and yet so pleased with its lessons, I find myself crying out with my heart, though my preaching voice is muted, "I desire to do your will, O my God; your law is within my heart. . . . I do not [want to] conceal your love and your truth from the great assembly" (Ps. 40:8, 10 NIV).

Here, then, my jealousy of the strutting roses finds contentment: that I shall bloom again according to the same providence that has attended my pruning. Pope John Paul II, Barbara Bush, and Olympiad are lovely in their spring debutant ball, but soon I shall join them again as Christ, who creates their beauty, also sends his redemptive sap through my parts and I rise to proclaim in the assembly, in the seminary, and in my heart, "You are my help and my deliverer" (Ps. 40:17). Yet I also recite the final line: "Do not delay, O my God!"

Here then is my answer. Here then is my lesson. Here then is my hope, now and forevermore. Soon I will rise, I pray, from this porch and this affliction, to join brothers in the battle. But for now, I ponder the glory of the resurrection in a body of sickness, before the roses in bloom, in a rocking chair, like some old withering soldier, with a heart rate too low, but with a Christ who is in full control of all of his creation. *Amen.*

NOTES

Preface

1. "Where is God my Maker, who gives songs in the night?" (Job 35:10).

Acknowledgments

1. James Stewart, *James Stewart: Walking with God*, ed. Gordon Grant (Vancouver: Regent College Publishing, 2006), 189.

Chapter One: A Theology of Thorns

1. C. H. Spurgeon, *Morning by Morning*, Hendrickson Christian Classics (Peabody, MA: Hendrickson Publishers, 2006), morning devotions for March 4.

2. Simon Kistemaker, *Exposition of the Second Epistle to the Corinthians* (Grand Rapids: Baker Books, 1997), 416.

3. See the best study on the subject, "Charles Haddon Spurgeon: Preaching Through Adversity," by John Piper, at http://www.founders.org/journal/fj23/article1.html (accessed March 21, 2010).

4. See Mother Teresa and Brian Kolodiejchuk, *Mother Teresa: Come Be My Light: The Private Writings of the "Saint of Calcutta"* (New York: Doubleday, 2007), 281.

5. I do not endorse Teresa's theology in order to see the principle at work in her life.

6. Martin Luther, "A Mighty Fortress Is Our God," *Trinity Hymnal* (Atlanta: Great Commission Publications, 1990), no. 92.

7. John of the Cross, *The Dark Night of the Soul*, ed. Benedict Zimmerman (Greenwood, SC: Attic Press, 1973).

8. Colonel Roger Dean Ingvalson's life is chronicled by the Library of Congress at http://lcweb2.loc.gov/diglib/vhp-stories /loc.natlib.afc2001001:09773 (accessed March 20, 2010).

9. Samuel Wilkes, as quoted in Derek Prime, *Let's Study 2 Corinthians* (Edinburgh: Banner of Truth, 2000), 176.

10. Jeremiah Burroughs, *Rare Jewel of Christian Contentment* (Edinburgh: Banner of Truth Trust, 1964), 19.

11. Ibid.

12. "For the sake of Christ, then, I am content with weaknesses, insults, hardships, persecutions, and calamities. For when I am weak, then I am strong" (2 Cor. 12:10).

13. Eugene Bartlett, "Victory in Jesus," *Baptist Hymnal*, 1975 ed. (Nashville: Convention Press, 1975), no. 475.

14. Personal letter from Mrs. Kelly Stultz to the author, August 27, 2007.

15. Twila Paris, "This Thorn" (Mountain Spring Music, Ariose Music, 1990). Used by permission.

Chapter Two: The Lord of the Storm

1. *Matthew Henry's Commentary on the Whole Bible*, ver. 5 (Old Tappan, NJ: Fleming Revell, n.d.), 491.

2. Neil Young, "My Boy" (Interscope Records, Silver Fiddle Music, 2000).

3. Catherine Marshall, *A Man Called Peter: The Story of Peter Marshall* (New York: McGraw-Hill, 1951), 114.

4. Ibid.

5. Dan Fogelberg, "The Reach" (Hickory Grove Music, 1981). Used by permission of Hal Leonard Corporation.

6. For instance, the term *nave* (of a church) comes from the French *nef*, meaning "a ship," according to Auguste Brachet and G. W. Kitchin, *An Etymological Dictionary of the French Language* (Oxford: Clarendon Press, 1873), 265. See also the excellent page on symbols in the early church: http://www.jesuswalk.com/christian-symbols/ship.htm (accessed March 27, 2010).

7. William L. Lane, *The Gospel According to Mark: The English Text with Introduction, Exposition, and Notes* (Grand Rapids: Eerdmans, 1974), 235.

8. Mark 6:53–56.

9. *No Time for Sergeants*, Warner Brothers Pictures, 1958.

10. *Matthew Henry's Commentary on the Whole Bible*, ver. 5 (Old Tappan, NJ: Fleming Revell, n.d.), 491.

11. William Barclay, *The Gospel of Mark*, New Daily Study Bible (Louisville: Westminster John Knox Press, 2001), 186.

12. C. S. Lewis, "The Horse and His Boy," illustrated by Pauline Baynes, in *The Chronicles of Narnia*, 1st one-volume ed. (New York: HarperCollins Publishers, 2004), 306.

13. Barclay, *The Gospel of Mark*, 186.

14. Grady Nutt and Paul Duke, "We, O God, Unite Our Voices," the Crescent Hill Hymn of Crescent Hill Baptist Church, Louisville, KY (1981). Used with permission.

15. R. T. France, *The Gospel of Mark: A Commentary on the Greek Text*, New International Greek Testament Commentary (Grand Rapids: Eerdmans, 2002), 259.

16. Michael Anthony Milton, "Your Sovereign Grace," *He Shall Restore* (Chattanooga: Music for Missions, 2005), CD.

Chapter Three: Finding God in Spiritual Depression

1. David Martyn Lloyd-Jones, *Spiritual Depression: Its Causes and Cure* (Grand Rapids: Eerdmans, 1965).

2. Frederick Buechner, *Telling Secrets* (San Francisco: HarperSanFrancisco, 1991), 2, 7–8.

3. See M. Craig Barnes, *When God Interrupts: Finding New Life Through Unwanted Change* (Downers Grove, IL: InterVarsity Press, 1996), 32.

4. John Piper, "Charles Spurgeon: Preaching Through Adversity," in *Bethlehem Baptist Church Conference for Pastors* (Minneapolis: Bethlehem Baptist Church, 1995). See http://www.founders.org/FJ23/article1.html. The article is adapted from a paper delivered at the Bethlehem Conference for Pastors, January 31, 1995.

5. See, for instance, James King, *William Cowper: A Biography* (Durham, NC: Duke University Press, 1986); John Piper, *The Hidden Smile of God: The Fruit of Affliction in the Lives of John Bunyan, William Cowper, and David Brainerd*, The Swans Are Not Silent (Wheaton, IL: Crossway Books, 2001).

6. Stanton Peele, "Why No Reduction in Depression in America," *Hartford Courant*, July 7, 2003.

7. Lloyd-Jones, *Spiritual Depression*. See chapter 1.

8. John Calvin, *Commentary on the Book of Psalms*, trans. James Anderson (Accordance Bible Software, 8.4.4), commentary on the title of Psalm 42.

9. Charles Haddon Spurgeon, *The Treasury of David* (Accordance Bible Software 8.4.4), introduction to Psalm 42.

10. Margaret Clarkson, "O Father, You Are Sovereign" (Hope Publishing, 1982). Used by permission.

11. M. Craig Barnes, *When God Interrupts: Finding New Life Through Unwanted Change* (Downers Grove, IL: InterVarsity Press, 1996), 146–47.

12. Joseph Scriven, "What a Friend We Have in Jesus," *Trinity Hymnal* (Atlanta: Great Commission Publications, 1990), no. 629.

Chapter Four: A Doxology in the Darkness

1. Thomas Watson, *A Divine Cordial* (Grand Rapids, MI: Sovereign Grace Publishers, 1971), 6.

2. This premise is propounded very well in John Guest, *In Search of Certainty* (Ventura, CA: Regal Books, 1983).

3. James Stewart, *James Stewart: Walking with God*, ed. Gordon Grant (Vancouver: Regent College Publishing, 2006), 118.

4. Brennan Manning, *Ruthless Trust: The Ragamuffin's Path to God* (San Francisco: HarperSanFrancisco, 2000), 5.

5. See Michael A. Milton, *Oh, the Deep, Deep Love of Jesus: Expository Messages from John 17* (Eugene, OR: Wipf and Stock Publishers, 2007).

6. Though some prefer "the prayer of consecration." See Leon Morris, *The Gospel According to John*, rev. ed. (Grand Rapids: Eerdmans, 1995), 634.

7. Alexander Maclaren, *Expositions of Holy Scripture*, St. John chapters XV to XXI (Grand Rapids: Eerdmans, 1982), 188.

8. *Pisteuo*: "to entrust to another." See the word appearing in *The Analytical Greek Lexicon* (London: Samuel Bagster and sons, n.d.; Accordance Bible Software); Milton, *Oh, the Deep, Deep Love of Jesus*, 93.

9. H. Richard Niebuhr, *Christ and Culture*, expanded ed. (San Francisco: HarperSanFrancisco, 2001).

10. Leon Morris, "John," in *The NIV Study Bible*, ed. Kenneth L. Barker (Grand Rapids: Zondervan, 2002; Accordance Bible Software 8.4.6), at 17:10.

11. Ibid.

12. Manning, *Ruthless Trust*, 18.

13. Ibid, 27.

14. Eugene H. Peterson, *The Message: Psalms* (Colorado Springs, CO: NavPress, 1994), 187.

15. See Job 1:7–11.

16. Manning, *Ruthless Trust*, 37.

17. Nicholas Wolterstorff, *Lament for a Son* (Grand Rapids: Eerdmans, 1987), 52. The reference is also found in David Calhoun's essay, "Poems in the Park: My Cancer and God's Grace," in *Suffering and the Goodness of God*, ed. Christopher W. Morgan and Robert A. Peterson (Wheaton, IL: Crossway Books, 2008), 196.

Chapter Five: Hannah's Faith

1. Leviticus 23:39–43.

2. Deuteronomy 16:13–15.

3. Matthew Henry and Thomas Scott, *A Commentary upon the Holy Bible, ver. 2, Joshua to Esther* (London: Religious Tract Society, 1835), 126.Notes

Chapter Seven: The Grace of Locust Shells, or How God Redeems the Pain of Our Past

1. As quoted in James Stewart, *James Stewart: Walking with God*, ed. Gordon Grant (Vancouver: Regent College Publishing, 2006), 208.

2. Grant Clarke and George W. Meyer, "In the Land of Beginning Again," in *The Bells of St. Mary's* (film).

3. Luder G. Whitlock and others, eds., *New Geneva Study Bible: Bringing the Light of the Reformation to Scripture: New King James Version* (Nashville: T. Nelson, 1995), 1382.

4. My first compact disc recording of original music was entitled "He Shall Restore," based on Joel 2:25. The title cut begins, "When the locusts came they caught me unaware." To listen, go to Michael Anthony Milton on iTunes and search for the album or song by name. Or see Michael Anthony Milton, *He Shall Restore* (Chattanooga: Music for Missions, 2005), CD.

5. See Revelation 3:12 and 21:2, but also Hebrews 12:22: "But you have come to Mount Zion and to the city of the living God, the heavenly Jerusalem, and to innumerable angels in festal gathering."

6. Such devastation is still not uncommon. Accounts of locust damage have been documented all over the world. See David Prior, *The Message of Joel, Micah, and Habakkuk: Listening to the Voice*

of God, The Bible Speaks Today (Downers Grove, IL: InterVarsity Press, 1998), 22–23. While we often think of locust plagues happening in Africa or Asia, the *New York Times* of September 9, 1895, recorded a locust plague that attacked the Maples of New York and New England. See http://query.nytimes.com/mem/archive-free /pdf?_r=1&res=950DE4DE113AE533A2575AC0A96F9C94649ED7CF.

7. See the commentaries that have nourished this message: James Montgomery Boice, *The Minor Prophets: An Expositional Commentary* (Grand Rapids: Zondervan, 1983); Thomas Edward McComiskey, *The Minor Prophets: An Exegetical and Expository Commentary*, 3 vols. (Grand Rapids: Baker Book House, 1992); Hans Walter Wolff and S. Dean McBride, *Joel and Amos: A Commentary on the Books of the Prophets Joel and Amos*, Hermeneia (Philadelphia: Fortress Press, 1977).

8. Margaret Clarkson "O Father, You Are Sovereign" (Hope Publishing, 1982). Used by permission.

9. Prior, *The Message of Joel*, 68.

10. See his speech at http://www.historyplace.com/speeches/ churchill-hour.htm, or hear the climactic, soaring rhetoric of Prime Minister Churchill at http://easylink.playstream.com /historyplace/thp-churchill-hour.rm.

11. Prior, *The Message of Joel*, 68.

12. George Bennard, "The Old Rugged Cross" (1913).

Chapter Eight: A Christ for Crippled Lambs and Lame Priests

1. As quoted in C. J. Mahaney, *Humility: True Greatness* (Sisters, OR: Multnomah, 2005), 66.

2. "Thus saith the Lord, Stand ye in the ways, and see, and ask for the old paths, where is the good way, and walk therein, and ye shall find rest for your souls" (Jer. 6:16 kjv).

3. See, for example, Caleb Thomas Winchester, *The Life of John Wesley* (Charleston, SC: BiblioLife, 2008).

4. Edmund P. Clowney, *Called to the Ministry* (Phillipsburg, NJ: P&R Publishing, 1964).

5. This is an example of the importance of systematic theology in understanding the Bible. Systematic theology surveys the whole of the Word of God and identifies, classifies, and differentiates doctrines and truths. For example, there are, in the Bible, three

types of law: ceremonial law, which is fulfilled in Christ; theocratic law, or those laws related by God to Israel when the Lord himself governed his people directly, which are abrogated or fulfilled, since there is no more theocracy; and moral law, the Ten Commandments and other precepts and commandments, which continue. There are also three uses of the law: salvific, showing us that we need a Savior; civil, providing a code for government and the common good; and didactic or teaching (also called punitive, protective and pedagogical). This famous "third use of the law"—"pedagogical"— which John Calvin taught, teaches us how to live and brings us great blessing in the keeping of that law. There is no better little book to read on this than Book III of John Calvin, *Institutes of the Christian Religion: The First English Version of the 1541 French Edition*, trans. Elsie Anne McKee (Grand Rapids: Eerdmans, 2009). It is so lovely in its application of the law of God that it has been singled out as its own publication: John Calvin, *Golden Booklet of the True Christian Life*, trans. Henry J. Van Andel (Grand Rapids: Baker Books, 2004). See also Charles Partee, *The Theology of John Calvin* (Louisville: Westminster John Knox Press, 2008). For a good study of the Ten Commandments, see Michael Scott Horton, *The Law of Perfect Freedom* (Chicago: Moody Press, 1993). For one of the best systematic theology books, I recommend Robert L. Reymond, *A New Systematic Theology of the Christian Faith* (Nashville: T. Nelson, 1998). While that book is a textbook, Reymond's Westminster Confession of Faith outline is rooted in the historic Reformed faith and is extraordinarily useful in surveying the doctrines of the Bible.

6. For a fine overview of his thought, see Stephen J. Nichols, *J. Gresham Machen: A Guided Tour of His Life and Thought* (Phillipsburg, NJ: P&R Publishing, 2004).

7. See J. Gresham Machen, *God Transcendent*, ed. Ned B. Stonehouse (Edinburgh: Banner of Truth Trust, 1982), 14.

8. Andrew A. Bonar, *Robert Murray M'Cheyne: Memoir and Remains* (London: Banner of Truth Trust, 1966), 274.

Chapter Ten: Wounded in the House of Friends: What to Do When Christians Hurt You

1. Lewis B. Smedes, *Forgive and Forget: Healing the Hurts We Don't Deserve* (San Francisco: Harper and Row, 1984).

2. Tennessee Williams, *The Theatre of Tennessee Williams* (New York: New Directions Publishing, 1990), 526.

3. J. C. Ryle, *Expository Thoughts on the Gospels: St. Luke* (Cambridge, UK: James Clarke, 1969), 122.

4. Gene Edwards, *Crucified by Christians* (Beaumont, TX: Seed-Sowers/Christian Books Pub., 1995).

5. Matthew Henry, *Commentary on the Whole Bible* (Old Tappan, NJ: Fleming Revell, n.d.), 268.

6. Mark Water, *The New Encyclopedia of Christian Quotations* (Grand Rapids: Baker Books, 2001), 430.

7. Malcolm Muggeridge, *Christ and the Media* (Vancouver: Regent College Publishing, 2003), 25.

8. Newman Hall, *Gethsemane, or Leaves of Healing from the Garden of Grief* (Edinburgh: T. & T. Clark, 1891). See http://www.gracegems.org/books5/g08.htm.

Chapter Eleven: Oh, My Son!

1. Thomas N. Walters, "On Teaching William Faulkner's 'Was'," *English Journal* 55, no. 2 (1966), 182–88.

2. As quoted in "The Quotable Faulkner" at http://www.goodreads.com/author/quotes/3535.William_Faulkner?page=4.

3. William Faulkner, *Absalom, Absalom!* (New York: Random House, 1936).

4. William S. Plumer, "A Sad History of David's Child." See http://www.apuritansmind.com/TheChristianFamily/Plumer ChristopherSadHistory.htm (accessed January 25, 2010).

5. Patrick M. Morley, *Pastoring Men: What Works, What Doesn't, and Why It Matters Now More Than Ever* (Chicago: Moody Publishers, 2009), 40–42, 45.

6. *Matthew Henry's Commentary (Condensed)* (Accordance Bible Software, 7.1), at 2 Samuel 18:33.

7. Words and music by Luther B. Bridges. See http://www.hymnsite.com/lection/980524.htm (accessed January 25, 2010).

Chapter Twelve: Overcoming the Obstacles of Life

1. John Calvin, *Commentaries on the Book of Joshua*, trans. Henry Beveridge (Grand Rapids: Eerdmans, 1950), 34.

2. Marten H. Woudstra, *The Book of Joshua*, New International Commentary on the Old Testament (Grand Rapids: Eerdmans, 1981), 108.

3. For more on the archaeological evidences, as well as the description of the city, see Bryant Wood, "The Walls of Jericho: Archaeology Confirms: They Really Did Come a-Tumblin' Down" (March 1999). See http://www.answersingenesis.org/creation/v21/i2/jericho.asp (accessed May 21, 2010).

4. Woudstra, *The Book of Joshua*, 38.

5. Calvin writes of this one, "The words, at the same time, imply that it was not an ordinary angel, but one of special excellence. For he calls himself captain of the Lord's hosts, a term which may be understood to comprehend not merely his chosen people, but angels also." See Calvin, *Commentaries on the Book of Joshua*, 86.

6. *Matthew Henry's Commentary (Condensed)* (Accordance Bible Software, 7.1), at Joshua 5:13–15. Although Woudstra disagrees and sees this as an angel of the Lord, he admits that the figure is "superhuman" and causes Joshua to worship. He then goes on to show how this holiness is linked to the presence of God. In this way he draws nearer to seeing a manifestation of the preincarnate Christ. See Woudstra, *The Book of Joshua*, 105.

7. See John 21:1–18.

8. See Revelation 2–3. Jesus gave both commendation and warning to each church, except the persecuted church Smyrna, which received encouragement without admonition or correction (2:10), and Laodicea, which received a strong warning about her lukewarmness in the things of God. Yet even to Laodicea he said, "Those whom I love, I reprove and discipline" (3:19). Is this not a most kind and encouraging word to those in sin? Thus Christ, as Matthew Henry says, gives us what our faith needs.

9. James Stewart, *James Stewart: Walking with God*, ed. Gordon Grant (Vancouver: Regent College Publishing, 2006), 128.

10. Woudstra, *The Book of Joshua*, 104.

11. Ibid, 112.

12. John Sammis and Daniel Towner, "Trust and Obey," *Trinity Hymnal* (Atlanta: Great Commission Publications, 1990), no. 672.

13. William Cowper, "God Moves in a Mysterious Way," *Trinity Hymnal*, no. 128.

14. Stephen E. Ambrose, *Comrades: Brothers, Fathers, Heroes, Sons, Pals* (New York: Simon & Schuster, 1999), 119.

15. David Harrell, *Out of the Depths* (Longwood, FL: Xulon Press, 2005), 29.

16. Ibid, 83.

Chapter Thirteen: God's Message to Spiritual Amputees

1. Timothy J. Keller, *The Reason for God: Belief in an Age of Skepticism* (New York: Dutton, 2008), 53–54.

2. See http://www.ehistory.com/uscw/features/medicine/cwsurgeon/amputations.cfm.

3. See Ephesians 6:10–20.

4. R. Kent Hughes, *Mark: Jesus, Servant and Savior*, vol. 2, Preaching the Word (Westchester, IL: Crossway Books, 1989), 37.

5. See R. C. Sproul and Keith Mathison, eds., *The Reformation Study Bible: English Standard Version* (Phillipsburg, NJ: P&R Publications, 2005), 1433.

6. Geoffrey Grogan, *Mark* (Fearn, Ross-shire, Scotland: Christian Focus, 1995), 131.

7. I am indebted to the insights of Kent Hughes.

8. A. W. Pink, *Studies in the Scriptures*, January 1932, p. 18.

9. Grogan, *Mark*, 131.

10. See http://www.spurgeon.us/index.php.

11. "'Miracle' Soldier Battling Back," *The Early Show*, CBS News website located at http://www.cbsnews.com/stories/2004/12/14/earlyshow/series/main660937.shtml, December 14, 2004.

Chapter Fourteen: The Grand Narrative

1. Philip Yancey, *Rumors of Another World* (Grand Rapids: Zondervan, 2003), 19.

2. See, for instance, P. Kyle McCarter Jr., "Exodus," in *Harper's Bible Commentary*, ed. James L. Mays (San Francisco: HarperSanFrancisco, 1988), 132.

RESOURCES FOR FURTHER STUDY

Allen, Leslie C. *The Books of Joel, Obadiah, Jonah, and Micah*. New International Commentary on the Old Testament. Grand Rapids: Eerdmans, 1976.

Ambrose, Stephen E. *Comrades: Brothers, Fathers, Heroes, Sons, Pals*. New York: Simon & Schuster, 1999.

Baptist Hymnal. 1975 ed. Nashville: Convention Press, 1975.

Barclay, William. *The Gospel of Mark*. New Daily Study Bible. Louisville: Westminster John Knox Press, 2001.

Barnes, M. Craig. *When God Interrupts: Finding New Life Through Unwanted Change*. Downers Grove, IL: Inter-Varsity Press, 1996.

Boice, James Montgomery. *The Minor Prophets: An Expositional Commentary*. Grand Rapids: Zondervan, 1983.

Bonar, Andrew A. *Robert Murray M'Cheyne: Memoir and Remains*. London: Banner of Truth Trust, 1966.

Brachet, Auguste, and G. W. Kitchin. *An Etymological Dictionary of the French Language*. Oxford: Clarendon Press, 1873.

Buechner, Frederick. *Telling Secrets*. San Francisco: HarperSanFrancisco, 1991.

Burroughs, Jeremiah. *Rare Jewel of Christian Contentment*. Edinburgh: Banner of Truth Trust, 1964.

Calvin, John. *Commentaries on the Book of Joshua*. Translated by Henry Beveridge. Grand Rapids: Eerdmans, 1950.

————. *Commentary on the Book of Psalms*. Edited by James Anderson. Accordance Bible Software, 8.4.4.

————. *Golden Booklet of the True Christian Life*. Translated by Henry J. Van Andel. Grand Rapids: Baker Books, 2004.

————. *Institutes of the Christian Religion: The First English Version of the 1541 French Edition*. Translated by Elsie Anne McKee. Grand Rapids: Eerdmans, 2009.

Clarke, George, and Grant W. Meyer. "In the Land of Beginning Again," in *The Bells of St. Mary's*. Film, 1946.

Clowney, Edmund P. *Called to the Ministry*. Phillipsburg, NJ: P&R Publishing, 1964.

Edwards, Gene. *Crucified by Christians*. Beaumont, TX: SeedSowers/Christian Books Pub., 1995.

Faulkner, William. *Absalom, Absalom!* New York: Random House, 1936.

Fogelberg, Dan. "The Reach," from the album *The Innocent Age*. Sony BMG Music Entertainment, 1985.

France, R. T. *The Gospel of Mark: A Commentary on the Greek Text*. New International Greek Testament Commentary. Grand Rapids: Eerdmans, 2002.

Garland, David E. *Mark*. NIV Application Commentary. Grand Rapids: Zondervan, 1996.

Grogan, Geoffrey. *Mark*. Fearn, Ross-shire, Scotland: Christian Focus, 1995.

Guest, John. *In Search of Certainty*. Ventura, CA: Regal Books, 1983.

Harrell, David. *Out of the Depths*. Longwood, FL: Xulon Press, 2005.

Henry, Matthew, Leslie F. Church, and Gerald W. Peterman. *The NIV Matthew Henry Commentary in One Volume: Based on the Broad Oak Edition*. Grand Rapids: Zondervan, 1992.

Horton, Michael Scott. *The Law of Perfect Freedom*. Chicago: Moody Press, 1993.

Hughes, R. Kent. *Mark: Jesus, Servant and Savior*. 2 vols. Preaching the Word. Westchester, IL: Crossway Books, 1989.

John of the Cross. *The Dark Night of the Soul*. Edited by Benedict Zimmerman. Greenwood, SC: Attic Press, 1973.

Keller, Timothy J. *The Reason for God: Belief in an Age of Skepticism*. New York: Dutton, 2008.

King, James. *William Cowper: A Biography*. Durham, NC: Duke University Press, 1986.

Kistemaker, Simon. *Exposition of the Second Epistle to the Corinthians*. Grand Rapids: Baker Books, 1997.

Lane, William L. *The Gospel According to Mark: The English Text with Introduction, Exposition, and Notes*. Grand Rapids: Eerdmans, 1974.

Lewis, C. S. *The Chronicles of Narnia*. Illustrated by Pauline Baynes. First one-volume edition. New York: HarperCollins Publishers, 2004.

Lloyd-Jones, David Martyn. *Spiritual Depression: Its Causes and Cure*. Grand Rapids: Eerdmans, 1965.

Machen, J. Gresham. *God Transcendent*. Edited by Ned B. Stonehouse. Edinburgh: Banner of Truth Trust, 1982.

Maclaren, Alexander. *Expositions of Holy Scripture*. Grand Rapids: Eerdmans, 1982.

Mahaney, C. J. *Humility: True Greatness*. Sisters, OR: Multnomah, 2005.

Manning, Brennan. *Ruthless Trust: The Ragamuffin's Path to God*. San Francisco: HarperSanFrancisco, 2000.

Marshall, Catherine. *A Man Called Peter: The Story of Peter Marshall*. New York: McGraw-Hill, 1951.

Matthew Henry's Commentary (Condensed). Accordance Bible Software, 7.1.

Matthew Henry's Commentary on the Whole Bible, ver. 5. Old Tappan, NJ: Fleming Revell, n.d.

McComiskey, Thomas Edward. *The Minor Prophets: An Exegetical and Expository Commentary*. 3 vols. Grand Rapids: Baker Book House, 1992.

Milton, Michael Anthony. *Authentic Christianity and the Life of Freedom: Expository Messages from Galatians*. Eugene, OR: Wipf and Stock Publishers, 2005.

───────. *Cooperation Without Compromise: Faithful Gospel Witness in a Pluralistic Setting*. Eugene, OR: Wipf and Stock Publishers, 2007.

───────. *Following Ben: Expository Preaching as the Power for Frail Followers of Pulpit Giants*. Eugene, OR: Wipf and Stock Publishers, 2006.

───────. *Follow Your Call*. Compact Disc Recording. Chattanooga: Music for Missions, 2008.

───────. *Giving as an Act of Worship*. Eugene, OR: Wipf and Stock Publishers, 2006.

───────. *Hit by Friendly Fire: What to Do When Christians Hurt You*. Eugene, OR: Wipf and Stock Publishers, 2008.

───────. *Leaving a Career to Follow a Call: A Vocational Guide to the Ordained Ministry*. Eugene, OR: Wipf and Stock Publishers, 1999.

───────. *Oh, the Deep, Deep Love of Jesus: Expository Messages from John 17*. Eugene, OR: Wipf and Stock Publishers, 2007.

───────. *Small Things, Big Things: Inspiring Stories of Everyday Grace*. Phillipsburg, NJ: P&R Publishing, 2009.

───────. *The Demands of Discipleship: Expository Messages from Daniel*. Eugene, OR: Wipf and Stock Publishers, 2005.

───────. "The Land of Beginning Again, Again." 2010. http://mikemilton.org/2010/04/24/the-land-of-begin ning-again-again [accessed May 12, 2010].

───────. *Through the Open Door*. Compact Disc Recording. Chattanooga: Music for Missions, 2011.

───────. *What God Starts, God Completes: Gospel Hope for Hurting People, The Life Lessons of Mike Milton*. Christian Focus, 2007.

───────. *What Is Perseverance of the Saints?* Phillipsburg, NJ: P&R Publishing, 2009.

───────. *What Is the Doctrine of Adoption?* Phillipsburg, NJ: P&R Publishing, 2012.

—————. "Your Sovereign Grace," from *He Shall Restore*. Compact Disc Recording. Chattanooga: Music for Missions, 2005.

"'Miracle' Soldier Battling Back." *The Early Show*, CBS News website located at http://www.cbsnews.com /stories/2004/12/14/earlyshow/series/main660937 .shtml, December 14, 2004.

Morgan, Christopher W., and Robert A. Peterson. *Suffering and the Goodness of God*. Wheaton, IL: Crossway Books, 2008.

Morley, Patrick M. *Pastoring Men: What Works, What Doesn't, and Why It Matters Now More Than Ever*. Chicago: Moody Publishers, 2009.

Morris, Leon. *The Gospel According to John*. Rev. ed. Grand Rapids: Eerdmans, 1995.

Nichols, Stephen J. *J. Gresham Machen: A Guided Tour of His Life and Thought*. Phillipsburg, NJ: P&R Publications, 2004.

Niebuhr, H. Richard. *Christ and Culture*. Expanded ed. San Francisco: HarperSanFrancisco, 2001.

Partee, Charles. *The Theology of John Calvin*. Louisville: Westminster John Knox Press, 2008.

Peele, Stanton. "Why No Reduction in Depression in America." *Hartford Courant*, July 7, 2003.

Peterson, Eugene H. *The Message: Psalms*. Colorado Springs, CO: NavPress, 1994.

Piper, John. "Charles Spurgeon: Preaching Through Adversity." In *Bethlehem Baptist Church Conference for Pastors*. Minneapolis: Bethlehem Baptist Church, 1995. See http ://www.desiringgod.org/resource-library/biographies /charles-spurgeon-preaching-through-adversity.

—————. *The Hidden Smile of God: The Fruit of Affliction in the Lives of John Bunyan, William Cowper, and David Brainerd*. The Swans Are Not Silent. Wheaton, IL: Crossway Books, 2001.

Prime, Derek. *Let's Study 2 Corinthians*. Edinburgh: Banner of Truth, 2000.

Prior, David. *The Message of Joel, Micah, and Habakkuk: Listening to the Voice of God*. The Bible Speaks Today. Downers Grove, IL: InterVarsity Press, 1998.

Reymond, Robert L. *A New Systematic Theology of the Christian Faith*. Nashville: T. Nelson, 1998.

Smedes, Lewis B. *Forgive and Forget: Healing the Hurts We Don't Deserve*. San Francisco: Harper & Row, 1984.

Sproul, R. C., and Keith Mathison, eds. *The Reformation Study Bible: English Standard Version*. Phillipsburg, NJ: P&R Publications, 2005.

Spurgeon, C. H. *Morning by Morning*. Hendrickson Christian Classics. Peabody, MA: Hendrickson Publishers, 2006.

—————. *Treasury of David*. 1869. Accordance Bible Software, 8.4.4.

Stewart, James. *James Stewart: Walking with God*. Edited by Gordon Grant. Vancouver: Regent College Publishing, 2006.

Teresa, Mother, and Brian Kolodiejchuk. *Mother Teresa: Come Be My Light: The Private Writings of the "Saint of Calcutta."* New York: Doubleday, 2007.

Trinity Hymnal. Atlanta: Great Commission Publications, 1990.

Walters, Thomas N. "On Teaching William Faulkner's 'Was'." *English Journal* 55, no. 2 (1966): 182–88.

Watson, Thomas. *A Divine Cordial*. Grand Rapids, MI: Sovereign Grace Publishers, 1971.

Whitlock, Luder G., R. C. Sproul, Bruce K. Waltke, and Moisés Silva, eds. *New Geneva Study Bible: Bringing the Light of the Reformation to Scripture: New King James Version*. Nashville: T. Nelson, 1995.

Winchester, Caleb Thomas. *The Life of John Wesley*. Charleston, SC: BiblioLife, 2008.

Wolff, Hans Walter, and S. Dean McBride. *Joel and Amos: A Commentary on the Books of the Prophets Joel and Amos*. Hermeneia. Philadelphia: Fortress Press, 1977.

Wolterstorff, Nicholas. *Lament for a Son*. Grand Rapids: Eerdmans, 1987.

Wood, Bryant. "The Walls of Jericho: Archaeology Confirms: They Really Did Come a-Tumblin' Down." March 1999. http://www.answersingenesis.org/creation/v21/i2/jericho.asp (accessed May 21, 2010).

Woudstra, Marten H. *The Book of Joshua*. New International Commentary on the Old Testament. Grand Rapids: Eerdmans, 1981.

About Reformed Theological Seminary

Founded in 1966, Reformed Theological Seminary was established to provide solid pastoral training grounded in a commitment to the authority of Scripture and the theological understanding of the Bible found in the Westminster Confession of Faith and the larger and shorter catechisms. Independently governed by a board of trustees, RTS serves students from over sixty evangelical denominations and churches. The seminary does not accept any government funding to assure its fidelity to its founding principles.

The first campus was located in Jackson, Mississippi, with additional campuses being established in later years in Orlando, Charlotte, Atlanta, and Washington, D.C. In addition to these campuses, RTS now has extension campuses in Memphis and Houston, and we offer an online master's degree from our virtual campus that serves students in countries throughout the world.

RTS is known for its academic rigor, effective pastoral preparation, commitment to missions, and flexible delivery systems and program accessibility. A bounty of information about our campuses and degree programs is available online at www.rts.edu.